KT-568-809

BA1

WITHDRAWN

The Which? Guide to Starting Your Own Business

Moreton Morrell Site

Warwickshire College

00525184

About the author

Anthony Bailey is a freelance journalist who specialises in consumer issues, personal finance and legal rights. He previously worked in the Money Group at Consumers' Association. He has contributed to many *Which?* books and edits the annual *Which? Way to Save Tax*. Anthony Bailey has written for a wide range of national newspapers and magazines, and writes the *Troubleshooter* column in the *Daily Express* and *Sunday Express*.

The Which? Guide to Starting Your Own Business

Anthony Bailey

WARWICKSHIRE
COLLEGE
LIBRARY

WARWICKSHIRE COLLEGE
LIBRARY

Class No:
658 · 11

Acc No:
005 25184

WHICH?
BOOKS

CONSUMERS' ASSOCIATION

WARWICKSHIRE COLLEGE
LIBRARY

Class No:
658.11

Acc No:
00525184

Which? Books are commissioned and researched by
Consumers' Association and published by
Which? Ltd, 2 Marylebone Road, London NW1 4DF
Email address: books@which.net

Distributed by The Penguin Group:
Penguin Books Ltd, 80 Strand, London WC2R 0RL

First edition (as *Starting Your Own Business*) 1983
Fifth edition March 2003

Copyright © 1983, 1984, 1985, 1986, 1988, 1991, 1992, 1993, 1994, 1996, 1998, 1999, 2003 Which? Ltd

British Library Cataloguing in Publication Data
A catalogue record for this book is available from the British Library

ISBN 0 85202 930 6

No part of this publication may be reproduced or transmitted in any form or by any
means, electronically or mechanically, including photocopying, recording or any
information storage or retrieval system, without prior permission in writing from the
publisher, nor be otherwise circulated in any form of binding or cover other than that
in which it is published and without a similar condition being imposed on the
subsequent purchaser. This publication is not included under licences issued by the
Copyright Agency.

For a full list of Which? books, please call 0800 252100, access our website at
www.which.net, or write to Which? Books, PO Box 44, Hertford SG14 1SH.

Editorial and production: Joanna Bregosz, Joanna Chisholm, Robert Gray, Nithya Rae
Original cover concept by Sarah Harmer

Typeset by Saxon Graphics Ltd, Derby
Printed and bound in Great Britain by Clays Ltd, St Ives plc

Contents

WARWICKSHIRE COLLEGE LIBRARY

Contents

★ An asterisk next to the name of an organisation in the text indicates that the address or contact details can be found in this section

Introduction

You may wonder why anyone would ever think of setting up in business when you discover what the odds are against making a success of it. Many new businesses go under in their first year. A majority will have failed within two or three years. But the statistics also reveal that many new businesses do prosper. Will you be a winner or a loser?

There is no secret winning formula. Every business venture is a risk. Indeed, risk is part of the attraction of running your own business compared with the relative safety of working for someone else. However, the risk can be minimised. There are two key elements to improving your chance of coming out on top: thorough preparation before you start and a sound financial backing for the business.

The Which? Guide to Starting Your Own Business is aimed anyone who is taking the first step in setting up their venture: whether you are someone using existing skills to form a simple one-person business (for example, being a self-employed hairdresser, chauffeur, plumber or consultant), or someone who has higher ambitions (setting up, say, a manufacturing, retailing or export business and possibly employing other people).

You need not be alone when you set out in business. There are many sources of official support. The government is keen to encourage and promote business start-ups and what it calls SMEs – small and medium-sized enterprises. These are businesses that are less than 25 per cent foreign-owned, and have no more than 49 employees for small businesses or 249 employees for medium-sized businesses. Knowing how to tap these sources of information is vital if your project is to succeed. In addition to providing you with the basic guidance you need, this book shows you how to do this and get relevant advice.

For example, government assistance is channelled through a range of agencies. The main co-ordinating body is the Department of Trade and Industry (DTI), so in many cases, the DTI is a good starting point. The guide tells you what the department's most useful publications, helplines and websites are. Moreover, the book sets out all the important legislation in this area, and helps you navigate through recent changes in the law and avoid the pitfalls in order to give yourself the best chance of success.

With so many challenges to face as you set up in business, it is sometimes easy to lose sight of the rewards of setting up on your own. But you are likely to acquire valuable experience – far broader than any gained as an employee – which is likely to stand you in good stead whether self-employment proves a long-term option or a short-term expedient. Even those upon whom self-employment was forced, through redundancy or unemployment, may find unexpected compensations for all the hard work: variety instead of routine; the realisation of your potential for self-deter-mination; and, when things work out well, the high of knowing you made it happen.

Chapter 1

Being prepared

To run your own business, of whatever kind, you need not only some capital and some capability but also a certain flair, toughness and good fortune. Very few of the people who start a small business have enough of both flair and luck to end up as millionaires. You might be one of them. Managing a business is rarely an easy option, especially to begin with – many start-up businesses fail in their first few years, often due to poor preparation. Many other businesses do not begin to make a profit until the third or fourth year of trading and it can take many long hours of work to get to that stage. Do you have what it takes to succeed?

- **Motivation** Your ambition must be to succeed in making a living that can support the standard of living, lifestyle and quality of life you desire. Many people who set up on their own are happy to accept a lower material standard of living in exchange for a different lifestyle or quality of life. The desire to escape your current job or unemployment may not be enough to achieve a prosperous business.
- **Focus** You should define your field of operations as specifically as possible, and be clear about your ultimate aims. If your dream is to start a business in one area and then expand elsewhere, or even to build up a great organisation, you must be sure to choose a business that is capable of such growth. If, however, your sole wish is to make a comfortable living and sell or close down the firm when you retire, choose a modest type of business that fits the bill.
- **Capacity to work hard** You may find yourself working for a harder taskmaster than any you have had previously, one who offers unlimited working hours, uncertain holidays and perhaps less money than you were earning before – at least to start with.

- **Self-reliance** You will be exchanging the support and companionship of fellow workers for a kind of isolation in which you stand or fall by your own decisions. There may be few perks – initially at least. You have to find the finance for things that may previously have been provided by an employer – learning new skills, sick pay, holiday pay, life insurance, pension.
- **Support** Ideally, your family should feel as committed as you. Their moral and even work support may be invaluable, especially during periods of difficulty. They must understand that their security depends on your success, that you may have less time for family life, and that the financial rewards may be some time in coming.

In addition, and among other subjects covered in this book, you'll need:

- adequate finance (see Chapter 2)
- a sound business plan (see Chapter 3)
- a suitable business structure (see Chapter 4)
- a way of reaching potential customers (see Chapter 6)
- orderly accounts (see Chapter 7)
- an understanding of tax (see Chapter 8)
- a way of getting your customers to pay (see Chapter 16).

Broadly, your choice of business venture will be one or a combination of:

- manufacturing a product
- providing a service
- distribution – selling a product or service.

Your choice depends on your marketable skills and which of them you want to be the foundation of your new career. You may want to capitalise on your existing knowledge and experience of a trade and on your training and qualifications. Or you may prefer to abandon your existing type of work to go in a completely new direction.

Developing a skill

A hobby in which you have some expertise – for example, cabinet-making, cooking, dressmaking, website design – may be the start of a successful business, especially if you have already begun to make money from it in your spare time. You will then have an incipient client list, and some idea of a potential market. When you approach a bank or other organisation for a loan, you will inspire more confidence, too. However, to make a full-time living from a skill is very different from doing it part-time, and indeed selling a hobby-item to a few friends and relatives may not be a good indication of its appeal to the general public or of its economic viability.

If your business project is not based on something you are doing already, consider starting off by making it into a spare-time pursuit while continuing with your job to get experience of the work.

Developing a new concept

You may have an original business idea. Perhaps you have designed a new product that fills a gap in the market, which everyone else has failed to notice; or you may have an idea for a service that would facilitate the workings of some industry.

Having developed an original business idea, you may not want to deal with the whole of the business side yourself – in which case, consider approaching a manufacturer about making your product, retaining for yourself any part of the operation (such as design or marketing) to which you can offer a unique contribution. If possible, protect any truly novel idea (for example, by applying for a patent) before disclosing it to any interested party.

Look around to see if you can find any other small firms working in the same or a related field, which might be willing to pool resources with you in a network. To set up such an arrangement you will have to do some research to find other firms in your line of trade in your locality. Consult your local Business Link* or the alternatives outside England (see below). See if there is a small business club in your area that could advertise your needs among its members.

Taking stock of your assets

The decision when to start will need to be related to the amount of money at your disposal. There is likely to be a period during which you will be paying all the outgoings, with little or no money coming in, while your own living expenses will still have to be met.

Begin by taking stock of your resources and assets, both human and financial. Human assets include your own skills and energy, and those of any member of your family who will be working with you.

Most people starting in business lack one or more of the basic skills needed for success. It is usually cheaper in the long run to buy in a missing skill, such as book-keeping, than to attempt every aspect of the business yourself. Not only will you take longer than a skilled person and make more mistakes, but also spending the same amount of time in using your own skill (selling, for example) will eventually make more money for the business.

Learning business skills

Certain skills, however, are worth learning, such as elementary accountancy and using a computer. If you intend to have a co-worker – perhaps your own husband, wife or partner – divide up between you who will learn what, at evening classes, through books or by correspondence course. This will be in addition to reading around the main subject of your enterprise.

Get used to the idea that, however knowledgeable you may become in your own field, there is still a lot to learn. Make sure that you take advantage of the various sources of help: a large number of 'Start your own business' training courses are available. Your local reference library may have information about local and national training opportunities. You may also find local evening classes that teach basic business skills, or, if you want more advanced training, you can take Open University courses or short courses at a local university or other college business school.

Where to get help and advice

Anyone who has previously always been an employee may find that making decisions without colleagues around is very difficult. Do not be too proud to ask for advice, preferably from those qualified to give it. You may have friends who have professional skills – accountants, bank managers, solicitors – and willing to advise you, perhaps initially without charging. You may have friends who are already successfully running a business and who may give you the benefit of their experience, provided you are not going to be in competition.

Governments have for many years emphasised the importance of fostering and facilitating enterprise and small businesses. As a result, they have encouraged the development of a web of organisations at national, regional and local level aimed at providing help and advice. The Department of Trade and Industry (DTI),* for example, provides a lot of useful information, particularly through its Small Business Service. Some of it applies across the UK and some more specifically to England. Government departments or agencies in Scotland, Wales and Northern Ireland can provide extra information for small businesses in their parts of the UK.

The DTI publishes booklets on many aspects of running a business, a full list of which is available through the DTI Publications Orderline.* Your local Business Link* or the alternatives outside England (see below) should also be able to supply you with copies or help you obtain them.

Business Links

Your nearest Business Link* (Small Business Gateway* in Scotland, Business Connect* in Wales, Invest Northern Ireland*) is the best first port of call for information about financial and practical help when you start a business. Business Links all offer both a business information service (at little or no cost) and business advice. Pricing structures for business advice vary from one Business Link to another, but are intended to be affordable to small businesses. Typically, a personal business adviser might undertake an initial business review free of charge and from then on provide subsidised consultancy.

Business advisers offer independent and confidential advice over a wide range of business-related matters from preparing a business plan to finding premises, from franchising to exporting and from patents to sources of finance. Business Links may also have office equipment such as computers and photocopiers, which you can use free or at a nominal charge. Where Business Links do not themselves offer a particular service, they can often refer you to an agency that does.

Local Enterprise Agencies

Local Enterprise Agencies, and Local Enterprise Companies in Scotland, can help support the small or new entrepreneur.

The address and telephone number of your nearest agency can be found through your Business Link★ or the alternatives outside England (see above) or in *Yellow Pages* under 'Business Enterprise Agencies'.

Local Enterprise Agencies are supported by partnerships between local industry and local and central government. They are independent organisations run mostly by experienced business people. They offer confidential and sometimes free counselling to people wishing to start a business. They can advise – or refer you to other advisers – on sources of finance, marketing, planning, training and finding premises. They may offer other initiatives to support local small businesses, such as business training and seminars and small business clubs. They may provide small workshop units run by a manager, employed by the enterprise agency or seconded from a company, who is available to help and advise the tenants.

Regional Development Agencies

Regional Development Agencies co-ordinate regional economic development, work to attract investment in the region, and support local business. They work closely with Business Links★ or the alternatives outside England (see above), which should remain your first point of contact for information about any government or European funding that may be available locally. It is worth asking what is available in your area before you embark on a project: once you have started, you may find it very hard to prove that you need help.

Regional selective assistance is a scheme aimed at attracting investment and encouraging employment by funding projects in most kinds of manufacturing industry and in some service industries. Grants of up to 15 per cent of the project costs are made for projects such as the opening of a new plant, or modernising or improving existing sites. The sorts of thing you can get a grant for include buying plant and machinery, buying and equipping the site and some associated one-off costs, such as professional fees. The amount of grant awarded will depend on the area, the needs of the project, the number of jobs safeguarded or created, and the impact the project will have on the economy. You will need to demonstrate that the project would not go ahead in the same form without the grant.

The Prince's Trust

The Prince's Trust* business start-up programme helps people aged between 18 and 30, many of them previously unemployed, to set up and run their own businesses. The Trust can provide advice and may give loans or bursaries to young people who have been unable to raise the finance they need elsewhere. Each new business is allocated a business monitor – a volunteer from the business community who offers help and advice for the first three years of trading. In addition, the Prince's Trust gives new businesses ongoing business support and marketing opportunities.

Shell LiveWIRE

Shell LiveWIRE* provides free local advice, information and business support to young people between 16 and 30 who are interested in setting up and running their own business. This help includes a free Essential Business Kit tailored to the enquirer's specific idea, and one-to-one advice from a local business adviser. In addition, there is an annual Young Business Start-up Awards competition, offering cash awards and help in kind through a series of county, regional and UK events.

Instant Muscle

Instant Muscle (IM)* is a charity specialising in helping people who are unemployed and particularly disadvantaged to start their own business. It provides free assistance with all aspects of business planning on an individual basis, can point you towards organisations that may be able to help with finance and gives up to 24 months' help after you start.

Chapter 2

Where to get financial backing

In order to prosper, all businesses need money whether it is in the form of start-up capital, working capital or short- or medium-term finance.

Start-up capital

Start-up capital is the once-and-for-all expenditure needed to set up a new business – the cash you must lay out before you have manufactured a single item or dealt with a single client. Unless you begin in your garage with a second-hand computer, you will have to pay for at least some of the following:

- premises – buying or rebuilding, conversion or even building from scratch
- plant and equipment, tools
- goodwill, if taking over an existing business
- office equipment and furniture
- installation of electricity, gas, telephone and any other services
- initial administrative costs: legal and other professional fees
- stationery: paper, envelopes, postcards, invoices, etc. printed with the firm's name
- publicity: cost of the initial launch
- insurance: for equipment, premises, liability (e.g., public and employers').

Assess this expenditure as accurately as possible and consider ways of reducing it if necessary: for example, by delaying the buying of any pieces of plant not immediately needed; or by leasing or hiring plant instead of buying.

Working capital

Working capital is the money you need to keep going during the interval between paying for your outgoings and getting the money in from your customers. In a manufacturing industry, some weeks or even months must pass before the products are finished, sold, despatched and paid for. In the meantime, you must keep paying for materials, labour and overheads. The cost of all of these represents your working capital needs.

Materials, stocks of finished products and labour costs will tie up money for a period before you get any returns. But, for example, if your suppliers give you 30 days' credit while your customers pay cash in seven days (in return for a small discount, perhaps), your working capital requirement will be reduced. At the same time, you will speed up your cash flow – the rate at which money passes out of and into your business. Working capital and cash flow are closely related: the more money you have lying stagnant – in materials, stock, or in customers' unpaid invoices – the more working capital you will need.

In the retail and distributive trades (for example, in a shop), goods held in stock represent the material costs. The amount of working capital needed and the rate of cash flow depend on the amount of unsold stock more than on unpaid invoices, because the retail trade has the advantage that customers generally pay straight away. A service industry, without stocks of materials or direct labour costs, needs comparatively little working capital – enough to pay overheads till the money starts coming in.

Short-term finance

Short-term finance is money required for short periods of time. It may be required for start-up capital or for temporary increases in working capital.

If you are setting up a service business or an agency or plan to be a middleman rather than a manufacturer, you may need little in the way of plant and labour. Consequently you'll need comparatively little start-up capital. But you may still need short-term money, to cover the interval between your outgoings and your receipts.

Such short-term finance can be in the form of a loan for a stated amount, generally with a fixed interest rate and repayment date. Or it could be an overdraft. An overdraft usually has a top limit beyond which you cannot borrow; interest is calculated on a daily basis and varies according to the prevailing base rate. An overdraft is usually one of the cheapest forms of borrowing even though there may be a setting-up charge. Its great disadvantage is that it is repayable on demand – though banks seldom call it in over the short term, as timing will usually have been agreed in advance.

Medium-term finance

This is money repayable in three to seven years. It is usually needed as start-up capital to pay for plant and equipment, but it may be required as working capital. Medium-term finance may be given at a fixed or variable rate of interest. If you can get a fixed-rate loan, you will lose out if interest rates fall but will have the advantage of stability. You know exactly how much you will have to pay for your loan, which is a help in making estimates. It is generally possible to repay a loan before it is due, but check whether there are any penalties for doing so. A variable-rate loan carries the risk that the rate may go up and put your financial forecasts in disarray.

Sources of outside finance

Money will usually be forthcoming for a sound project if well presented. If you cannot get the money you need, there may be a flaw in your plans or you may not have described them to the best advantage. Ask any contact you may have in the world of finance – your bank manager, accountant or other financial adviser – whether they know of anybody looking for an investment. Some people have found investors by advertising in the personal columns of newspapers, but do not hope for too much with this method.

Banks

The most obvious source of finance is a high-street bank. The major banks run some form of business advisory service, and many also publish booklets about starting a business. A bank may help you with a cash-flow forecast (see Chapter 3).

If you do not need regular access to a local branch, consider Internet and telephone banking to increase your choice of possible banks. Investment banks can also provide medium-term finance. If your project is closely associated with another country, an approach to one of that country's banks might attract satisfactory results.

Your own bank will have some confidence in you if you are generally solvent and in control of your outgoings and it is familiar with your financial history. Don't avoid your own bank fearing, for example, that a past unauthorised overdraft may be held against you. Approach the bank and two or three other potential lenders so that you can compare the different terms they offer.

Many banks have special schemes for helping new businesses: these include unsecured loan schemes, loans with capital repayment deferred and charge-free periods. However attractive the initial deal, you will be affected by the bank's charges for as long as you are with them. Scrutinise the standard tariff of charges and try negotiating a special tariff if you think the normal one looks expensive.

Offering security

A bank may lend without any security, but usually only on sound propositions where it is clear that the income generated will be enough to repay the loan. An overdraft is an option, but relying on overdrafts has its dangers. Although they are flexible and quick to arrange, overdrafts are repayable on demand. Banks can – and sometimes do – demand immediate repayment, leaving you little alternative to calling in the receivers.

Can you provide security, if required? A life insurance policy is unlikely to bring in much if you surrender it to raise capital for your business, but it may be acceptable as security for a bank loan. A property or land can provide security for a loan or overdraft if it is freehold or on a long lease (more than 21 years left, say). The bank's estimate of its value will be the figure that remains after you deduct the amount owing on a first mortgage, but it will probably make a further deduction to take into account what it might get on a quick sale. The bank will also need to ensure that anyone having an equitable interest in the home (a spouse or child over 18 living in the home, for example) has taken legal advice.

An alternative to consider would be selling your home and moving to a cheaper or rented home, to provide more start-up capital. If you intend to buy or rent a factory from a local authority, especially in a development area, this may secure you a high place on the housing list. You may feel that to part with the roof over the family's head is too rash, but lenders will expect you to carry a portion of the risk. However, it is easy in trying to raise capital for a project about which you are very enthusiastic to give too much security to your source of finance, leaving nothing for future borrowing.

Small Firms Loan Guarantee Scheme

The Small Firms Loan Guarantee Scheme is designed to assist viable small firms that are unable to raise conventional finance because of lack of security or track record. By providing a Government Guarantee against default by the borrower, it enables banks and other financial institutions to lend where they would normally be unable to do so. Lenders, however, make the final decision on whether to lend on the basis of having a guarantee.

The guarantee would cover 85 per cent of a maximum loan of £250,000 for established businesses, which have been trading for two years or more. For other businesses, the guarantee would cover 70 per cent of a maximum of £100,000. The loan term must be between two and 10 years. In return for providing the guarantee, the scheme charges the customer a premium of 0.5 per cent a year on a fixed-rate loan, 1.5 per cent on a variable-rate loan.

Loans are available for most business purposes, though there are some restrictions. Full information about this scheme can be obtained via a Business Link★ (or the alternatives outside England), from one of the participating lenders (including most high-street lenders) or from the DTI Small Business Service Loan Guarantee Unit.★

Leasing

Leasing is a form of obtaining medium-term finance without the need to borrow money. Your working capital is not tied up in rapidly depreciating machinery and you can reduce your borrowing requirements. The plant, equipment and vehicles you need are bought by a lessor such as a finance company and then leased to you for an agreed rent. At the end of the contract it is common for the leased equipment to be sold, and the greatest part of the proceeds (say 90 per cent) will then be returned to you as a rebate of rentals. Alternatively, you may be able to continue leasing the equipment at a reduced rental.

The lessor claims any available tax allowances such as capital allowances and this is reflected in the level of rental charges, which would otherwise be higher. The rent counts as an allowable business expense against tax, which you the lessee can offset against income tax, although there may be a ceiling on the amount you can claim for cars costing more than £12,000.

You have to specify exactly what equipment you want. The lessor buys it from the manufacturer and leases it to you on the agreed terms. They may ask you to establish your creditworthiness: for example, by providing a bank reference. No security other than the leased goods is usually required, though you may be asked to pay a few months' rental in advance.

You can sometimes lease vehicles and some office equipment for short periods and to exchange later for more up-to-date models. Check your contract carefully to see whether this would be possible and on what terms. If you are leasing the kind of equipment that needs regular servicing you may be offered a 'service-inclusive' contract. Compare such an offer with any available alternatives for separate leases and service contracts.

Many major providers of lease finance to industry and commerce in the UK are members of the Finance & Leasing Association.★ You can ask for a list of members to be sent to you. Most of them are London-based but operate in any part of the country. The Association produces an annual report, which gives an overview of the types of leasing business undertaken by members.

Hire-purchase

Hire-purchase is another way of obtaining plant and equipment without capital outlay. You pay a deposit and then regular fixed instalments. At the end of the contract you can pay a further fee to buy the goods outright. Instalment payments are generally higher than interest on a bank loan, but you may not wish to, or be able to, increase your bank loan. The counterbalancing advantage is that in a hire-purchase agreement the terms are normally fixed. Unlike a bank overdraft, charges cannot be increased if interest rates generally should rise (although you may find variable-rate deals for larger amounts). A *Guide to Hire Purchase and Leasing* is available free from the Finance & Leasing Association.★

British Venture Capital Association

The British Venture Capital Association (BVCA)★ represents companies offering venture capital – long-term finance for entre-preneurs who are ambitious to expand their companies. Most investments from venture-capital firms take the form of equity capital. Their returns are entirely dependent on the growth and profitability of the business. Venture-capital firms are more than just a source of finance. They often provide both financial and strategic support to enable new companies to develop into the major businesses of tomorrow. This involvement will vary from firm to firm, but day-to-day management control is not sought. The majority will expect to participate through a seat on the board.

The BVCA publishes *A Guide to Venture Capital* for entrepreneurs starting their own business or requiring additional capital. The guide will also help you to prepare a business plan to present when you have identified the most appropriate source of venture capital.

BVCA members tend to invest amounts over £100,000. Their names can be found in the Association's annual directory, which lists members' investment criteria and all their contact details. You can obtain a free copy from the BVCA. Having prepared a business plan, you should approach the most appropriate source of venture capital either directly or through an adviser. You may also want to look at *Sources of finance for your business*, available from the DTI Publications Orderline.★

The National Business Angels Network

Business angels are private individuals who usually invest in start-up and growth businesses, and they can be found through the National Business Angels Network (NBAN).★ This government-backed non-profit-making organisation acts as a catalyst and clearing house in bringing together entrepreneurs and business angels across the UK. It can help you to find funding, usually between £25,000 and £1,000,000. For start-up enterprises, business angels are likely to be more selective and may invest on more demanding terms. They are more likely to be interested if you have relevant business experience, a good business plan and realistic financial forecasts. They will take a percentage of the issued share capital and will usually offer managerial input too.

Businesses can register with NBAN for an annual fee of £100 plus VAT. Brief details are then placed on the NBAN website and in the monthly NBAN bulletin. Information can also be passed to other investor networks at your request. Businesses may also have the chance to make presentations to potential investors at local meetings. A local NBAN agent can help with the preparation of your business plan and entry on to the NBAN database (a fee will be charged for this). NBAN can send you an information pack and put you in touch with your nearest NBAN agent.

3i

3i plc* is a venture capital company (and member of the BVCA, see above). It invests in businesses across the whole business spectrum, from family firms to high-technology enterprises. It helps them at all stages of change: at start-up, when risk-capital may be required; during expansion; and later during phases of development, such as diversification, acquisition, management buy-out and management buy-in. 3i is a long-term investor, which subscribes for a minority share in businesses. Its investments are usually in excess of £500,000.

Enterprise Investment Scheme

The Enterprise Investment Scheme (EIS) is designed to attract individuals to invest relatively small amounts of capital in unquoted businesses trading in the UK. It works by giving investors tax relief when they buy newly issued shares in an unquoted trading company. Various types of business are excluded, for example companies in farming, market gardening, property development and the hotel business, which have significant property portfolios. To get the full amount of tax relief, the investor must hold the shares for at least three years if issued after 5 April 2000 (five years if issued before that date).

Investors can become paid directors of the company provided they have not been linked to the company before the shares were issued. The scheme is not open to employees or shareholders with more than 30 per cent of the shares.

An investor can get income tax relief at the starting rate of tax (currently 20 per cent) on up to £150,000 of investment in any one tax year. If the qualifying conditions are met, the proceeds arising from the disposal of the shares after three years or more are exempt from capital gains tax. If the shares realise a loss at that time, the investor can claim relief against income or capital gains tax.

If you are in any doubt about whether your company qualifies for the EIS, you should consult your accountant or tax inspector. You may also want to look at leaflet IR137 *The Enterprise Investment Scheme* from the Inland Revenue (ask your tax office).

Chapter 3

Drawing up a business plan

You have an idea for a business, but will it work? And will you be able to convince a bank or other source of finance that it will be successful? Most entrepreneurs will need some outside finance. If you are to raise the necessary money, you will have to give a potential lender a convincing business plan.

Each funding organisation has its own rules for considering a business plan. Prepare one carefully to satisfy their particular regulations. For some types of finance you must present a business proposal in a standard form, which may include an independent accountant's report. Lenders will want to know:

- what kind of business you intend to set up
- the kind and size of market you expect to trade in
- the likely extent of the competition
- how you propose to market your product or service
- a budget, profit-and-loss and cash-flow forecasts (see below) for at least 12 months, which will demonstrate that the loan can be repaid after all your business expenses have been met
- what (if any) relevant qualifications and experience you have
- whether you have sought expert advice
- what resources you have (e.g., redundancy money, savings, stocks and shares and other securities and investments, valuables convertible into cash, the value of your house and car)
- where the rest of the financing of your enterprise will come from, including other loans such as a loan from a member of the family at low interest
- how much you want to borrow, for how long and how you propose to pay it back
- whether you are asking for too little money – don't underestimate your requirements.

Banks and other financial institutions usually make a charge for setting up a loan or overdraft facility, generally of the order of at least 1 per cent (negotiated individually in each case). This should be allowed for in your planning calculations.

Using an accountant

Consider using an accountant at some stage, perhaps to help review your plan before you present it and to assist in the preparation of a cash-flow forecast. Make sure that you understand and believe in the assumptions and the calculations, because it is you who will have to explain and justify them to the bank manager or other potential lender and it will be your responsibility to produce the results to match them.

You must show that your forecasts are realistic and that you will monitor progress against them, week by week or month by month. Be ready to explain how you will cope if things don't go to plan. What provision have you made for slack times or unforeseen contingencies, such as a postal strike affecting business or an increase in the interest rate of a variable rate loan? The business plan is as much for your benefit as for that of a potential lender.

If you already know something about business accounting and revel in figures, you may think that you can do without an accountant. But however nimble with numbers you may be, you are unlikely to have an accountant's grasp of the innumerable regulations, experience in dealing with the Inland Revenue or all-round familiarity with different aspects of business. An accountant can help you to:

- decide whether to set up as a sole trader, partnership, limited company or co-operative
- find ways of raising capital
- set up profit-and-loss and cash-flow forecasts
- decide whether to register for VAT if you do not have to
- choose a starting date and a trading year-end date
- keep day-to-day records, account books and ledgers
- claim all possible allowances, expenses and reliefs against tax, and negotiate with the tax inspector
- fill in your tax return
- cope with pensions, annuities and insurance.

Choose an accountant carefully. Look for one with proper qualifications, such as FCA or ACA after their name. For tax advice, ATII or FTII denote members of the Chartered Institute of Taxation.★ Use *Yellow Pages* to find names and addresses. You can get a full list of chartered accountants in your area from your local District Society of Chartered Accountants. The Institute of Chartered Accountants in England and Wales★ publishes several useful booklets.

Costing your product or service

The cost of producing anything is made up of a number of elements. How many are involved depends on whether it is a product or service. You will want to do better than just break even and cover your costs. To find your selling price, add to your break-even figures an amount that will be your profit. Do the costing sums cautiously. Underestimating your costs or overestimating your likely production could make the difference between trading at a profit and a loss.

Overheads

Generally speaking, overheads are the standing costs of the business, which must be paid whether or not you succeed in making and selling anything. In the annual accounts, overheads are classified under the following headings:

- salaries and wages – the before-tax remuneration paid to office and sales staff, also directors' salaries and any other money drawn out of the business
- rent and rates
- heating, lighting and other services including gas, electricity, oil, propane gas, water and sewerage
- advertising/marketing – excluding the cost of any special launch
- printing, postage, stationery, telephone, fax – all office supplies and expenses
- motor and travel expenses – vehicle excise duty, insurance, servicing, repairs, petrol; expenses of travel by other means
- leasing and/or hire charges
- insurances

- professional fees – accountant, solicitor, patent agent
- depreciation – including motor vehicles
- interest on loans and overdraft
- sundry expenses.

Allow for overheads when you work out what to charge for a unit of your product or an hour of your time.

Estimate pessimistically the number of units of your product you will make and sell in your first year of full production given your present resources. The overheads cost per unit is the cost of all overheads in one year divided by the number of units of the product manufactured in that year. For example, if total overheads are £20,000 and the estimated production is 10,000 units, add £2 to the materials and labour cost of each unit to break even.

Direct labour costs

In a manufacturing business, direct labour costs are the before-tax wages paid to the people who actually make the product (not the wages of ancillary workers such as sales and office staff). The direct labour cost per unit is the cost of direct labour in one year divided by the number of units of the product manufactured in that year.

In practice, labour costs should be considered as overheads. They are largely fixed costs because it is difficult to hire workers only when you have orders for your product and lay them off when you have none.

Cost of materials

This is the price of the materials from which products are made. The materials cost per unit is the cost of materials in one year divided by the number of units of the product manufactured in that year. For a retailer or wholesaler, the materials are the stock of goods. An agent or consultant has no materials costs.

Costs in a service business

Instead of costing per unit of product, you cost per hour of the time spent by you or a member of your staff. Overheads usually represent the chief element of costs of the business. If you are, for example, a washing-machine engineer or a plumber, your charge should include travelling time and expenses, the cost of tools and equipment, and the wages of the person who answers the telephone and makes out the invoices – all these are overheads. And the chief element in the overheads will be salaries or wages, which have to be paid whether or not anyone is actually out on a job. To all this you must add your profit charge. When you do a job yourself, you should also charge for your time, and include a profit element.

If your total overheads come to £12,000 for an estimated total of 1,000 job-hours per year, your break-even price per hour will be £12. If you have to replace the washing machine's drum or motor, you will have to charge the customer separately for materials.

Financial forecasts

To work out the viability of your proposed business, you will need to make some financial forecasts. Will you have enough of your own money to make the business work and give you a reasonable profit? Or will you have to borrow money?

Profit-and-loss forecast

Any potential lender will want a profit-and-loss forecast. Choose a target – the amount of sales you think you can achieve in one year. Use as the break-even figure the minimum amount you require for your business and personal expenses, and decide how soon you have to reach that point. Not till then is the business moving into profit.

Your sales will need to increase steadily month by month in order to reach the target figure on time. Work out a set of projected monthly sales figures, and arrange them on a 12-month table.

Here's an example, though the same method would be used for any other kind of business. John runs a newly started, small-scale manufacturing business. He is confident of his market and plans to achieve sales of £50,000 a month by the end of the first year. VAT does not directly affect the calculation of business profits, so John does not include VAT in this forecast on either sales or purchases.

John draws up a profit-and-loss account (see Table A, below). He shows:

- **A** – estimated first-year sales receipts
- **B** – the cost of materials estimated as a percentage (50 per cent) of sales
- **C** – labour costs estimated as a percentage (30 per cent) of sales – he plans to use part-time labour in the first instance, building up to full-time employees as and when they can be justified
- **D** – gross profit, i.e. sales receipts minus materials and labour costs
- **E** – overheads – they vary from month to month but for this one-year profit-and-loss forecast it is legitimate to average them over 12 months
- **F** – the net monthly profit [or loss if in square brackets], i.e. gross profit minus overheads. If the figures follow this prediction, the business will break even at month 6, when it will be notionally trading at a profit.

If the business needs to borrow money, interest charges will reduce the net profit and John will need to amend the forecast.

As a sole trader (and not a company), John cannot claim his monthly drawings for his own living expenses as a salary and part of the firm's overheads. He will need to discuss his personal drawings with his lender. If he were trading as a limited company, he would pay himself a director's salary, which would be included in the overheads.

A single-person business in a service industry – say, a plumber – may have no materials or labour costs, only overhead expenses. The sales figures would be the same as gross profit figures. In a retail or wholesale business, the materials would be the purchases of stock.

Cash-flow forecast

However much profit you expect to be making by the end of the first year, your plans won't work if you cannot meet your suppliers' invoices or your overhead expenses – not to mention the living expenses of you and your family. A cash-flow forecast is essential. It must show when money is likely to flow into your business and when it is likely to flow out. A lender will examine your cash-flow forecast to assess your ability to control your financial resources.

A cash-flow forecast calculates the difference between your outgoings and your income. It is based on month-by-month

Table A John's estimated profit-and-loss forecast: figures in £000s [those in square brackets are minus figures]

month	% of sales	1	2	3	4	5	6	7	8	9	10	11	12	total
A sales receipts		1	3	6	10	15	20	25	30	35	40	45	50	280
B less materials purchased	50%	0.5	1.5	3	5	7.5	10	12.5	15	17.5	20	22.5	25	140
C less direct labour	30%	0.3	0.9	1.8	3	4.5	6	7.5	9	10.5	12	13.5	15	84
D gross profit	20%	0.2	0.6	1.2	2	3	4	5	6	7	8	9	10	56
E less overheads	17%	4	4	4	4	4	4	4	4	4	4	4	4	48
F net profit	3%	[3.8]	[3.4]	[2.8]	[2]	[1]	–	1	2	3	4	5	6	8

predictions (or educated guesses) about the times when you will be paying out and when you will be collecting money, over a period such as six months or a year. If receipts are lower than outgoings, you will have to cover the difference from funds available in reserve, or by bank overdraft or other forms of credit.

Receipts can be hard to predict. Sales may fluctuate from month to month. Some customers pay cash in seven days, usually expecting to be rewarded by a cash discount negotiated in advance. Others may arrange to pay in 30 or 60 days. Bad customers and bad debts mean part of your money may be outstanding for a long time – or for ever. You should allow an estimated sum for this in each month's calculations of receipts.

Outgoings are largely predictable and include:

- wages – the payment of which cannot be postponed
- materials – some suppliers insist on cash on delivery
- VAT – normally paid quarterly and, if appropriate, refunded to you quarterly
- overheads, such as major bills payable at different intervals, insurance once a year, rent, electricity, gas, telephone once a quarter, and so on – entered in the books as they are paid and making for an irregular pattern in your accounting, with several bills in some months, and none in others.

Will John be able to fund wages, materials and overheads during months when little or nothing is coming in? He draws up a cash-flow forecast (see Table B, below), using the same figures as in his profit-and-loss forecast but this time including VAT, which has an effect on the cash flowing in and out of the business. He shows:

- **a** opening amount of cash available or overdraft at the start of the month – for month 1 the total of payments, which is the maximum borrowing requirement (line **g**), exceeds both his capital and the family loan (line **h**), leaving the business with an overdraft at the end of month carried forward as the opening figure for month 2: by the end of month 2, the overdraft has increased to £10,720 carried forward to month 3 and so on
- **b** estimated monthly payments including VAT to suppliers, i.e. the cost of materials from the profit-and-loss forecast to be paid in cash if John has not yet become creditworthy

- **c** estimated monthly capital payments including VAT, i.e. plant and machinery and so on, which John reckons he can spread over the first six months
- **d** wages and salaries (including National Insurance contributions)
- **e** estimated monthly overhead payments including VAT where appropriate (e.g., VAT will be charged on advertising and stationery but not on rent and rates). Overheads were averaged out in the profit-and-loss forecast but the cash-flow forecast takes account of when the payments are actually made
- **f** VAT charged against the business in each quarter – the VAT figure is the amount that must be paid as determined by the date of the invoice and not by the date the money is received: John gives his customers one month to pay so, e.g., the sales credited in month 2 represent a VAT receipt in month 1 in which the goods were invoiced and delivered
- **g** estimated monthly amount that may have to be borrowed if there are no receipts, i.e. if no money comes into the business. Total payments in lines **b** to **f** are either deducted from an opening credit balance in line **a** or added to an opening overdraft in line **a**
- **h** John reckons that he needs about £15,000 to buy plant, machinery and office furnishing and can raise £7,000 from redundancy money and by selling his present car and leasing a small van and his father-in-law will lend him up to £5,000 interest-free if required to be repaid from profits. John bases his calculations on the same 12-month scheme as his profit-and-loss forecast, entering his £7,000 in line **h** in the first month
- **i** estimated monthly sales figures including VAT. John gives one month to pay so his first cash receipts come in month 2
- **j** estimated VAT refund
- **k** closing amount of cash available [or overdraft if in square brackets] at the end of the month. The maximum borrowing requirement in line **g** minus receipts in lines **h** to **j**: for month 1, John's borrowing requirement is £2,180; it rises each month until month 7 then falls and rises again before ending the year at £42,000.

Table B John's projected cash-flow forecast: figures in £000s [those in square brackets are minus figures]

month	1	2	3	4	5	6	7	8	9	10	11	12	13
a opening bank balance/overdraft	nil	[2.18]	[10.72]	[19.9]	[26.08]	[30.58]	[38.58]	[47.71]	[46.14]	[46.13]	[53.02]	[47.14]	[42.14]
PAYMENTS (inc VAT)													
b suppliers	0.59	1.76	3.53	5.88	8.81	11.75	14.69	17.63	20.56	23.5	26.44	29.38	29.38
c plant and machinery	2.35	5.88	2.35	1.18	2.35	3.53							
d wages and salaries (inc NI)	0.3	0.9	1.8	3.0	4.5	6.0	7.5	9.0	10.5	12.0	13.5	15.0	15.0
e overheads with VAT	2.94	1.18	3.53	3.53	0.59	2.35		1.18	1.18		1.18		
no VAT	8.0	8.0	1.5	5.0		2.0	8.0		3.0	5.0		3.5	8.0
f VAT office							2.44			7.52			11.63
g maximum borrowing requirement	[14.18]	[11.9]	[23.43]	[34.96]	[42.33]	[56.21]	[71.21]	[75.52]	[81.38]	[94.15]	[94.14]	[95.02]	[106.15]
RECEIPTS (inc VAT)													
h capital – John	7.0												
– family loan	5.0												
i sales	–	1.18	3.53	7.05	11.75	17.63	23.5	29.38	35.25	41.13	47.0	52.88	58.75
j VAT office				1.83									
k closing bank balance/ projected borrowing	[2.18]	[10.72]	[19.9]	[26.08]	[30.58]	[38.58]	[47.71]	[46.14]	[46.13]	[53.02]	[47.14]	[42.14]	[47.40]

Table C John's revised profit-and-loss forecast: figures in £000s [those in square brackets are minus figures]

month	% of sales	1	2	3	4	5	6	7	8	9	10	11	12	total
A sales receipts less VAT		3	6	10	15	20	25	30	35	35	40	40	40	299
B less materials purchased	50%	1.5	3	5	7.5	10	12.5	15	17.5	17.5	20	20	20	149.5
C less direct labour	30%	0.9	1.8	3	4.5	6	7.5	9	10.5	10.5	12	12	12	89.7
D gross profit	20%	0.6	1.2	2	3	4	5	6	7	7	8	8	8	59.8
E overheads	17.3%	4	4	5	4	4	5	4	4	5	4	4	5	52
F net profit	2.7%	[3.4]	[2.8]	[3]	[1]	–	–	2	3	2	4	4	3	7.8

35

The Which? Guide to Starting Your Own Business

36

Table D John's revised cash-flow forecast: figures in £000s [those in square brackets are minus figures]

month	1	2	3	4	5	6	7	8	9	10	11	12	13
a opening bank balance/overdraft	nil	[4.54]	[8.7]	[19.59]	[26.72]	[28.60]	[30.47]	[40.35]	[36.75]	[32.04]	[39.72]	[30.57]	[23.25]
PAYMENTS (inc VAT)													
b suppliers	1.76	3.53	5.88	8.81	11.75	14.69	17.63	20.56	20.56	23.5	23.5	23.5	23.5
c plant and machinery	2.35	1.18	2.35	1.18									
d wages and salaries (inc NI)	0.9	1.8	3.0	4.5	6.0	7.5	9.0	10.5	10.5	12.0	12.0	12.0	12.0
e overheads – with VAT	3.53	1.18	3.53		1.76			0.59	1.18		2.35	–	
– no VAT	8.0		2.0	5.0		2.0	8.0		3.0	5.0		3.0	8.0
– leasing			1.18			1.18			1.18			1.18	
f VAT office							4.63			8.31			9.97
g maximum borrowing requirement	[16.54]	[12.23]	[26.64]	[39.08]	[46.23]	[53.97]	[69.73]	[72.0]	[73.17]	[80.85]	[77.57]	[70.25]	[76.72]
RECEIPTS (inc VAT)													
h capital – John	7.0												
– family loan	5.0												
i sales	–	3.53	7.05	11.75	17.63	23.5	29.38	35.25	41.13	41.13	47.0	47.0	47.0
j VAT office				0.61									
k closing bank balance/ projected borrowing	[4.54]	[8.7]	[19.59]	[26.72]	[28.60]	[30.47]	[40.35]	[36.75]	[32.04]	[39.72]	[30.57]	[23.25]	[29.72]

John's profit-and-loss in Table A shows that he makes a profit of £8,000, but only if he does not need to borrow and pay interest. However, his cash-flow forecast in Table B indicates that he will indeed have to borrow. Borrowing drops after peaking in month 10, a promising trend. John adds a month 13 projection (in Table B) keeping purchases from suppliers steady at the month 12 level. But his overdraft increases again because of a VAT payment due in this month. He tries re-scheduling overheads or delaying payments but this makes no significant difference to his business.

He looks at ways of reducing all outgoings. Reduced purchases of materials will necessarily lower sales. He fixes on a less ambitious monthly sales figure of £40,000 but aims for a faster growth in sales, to achieve £40,000 in month 10 and break even in month 5. By leasing instead of buying some of the plant and machinery he can reduce his capital cash expenditure but will incur leasing charges on which VAT is payable. He needs to re-schedule some of the outgoings but feels it would be unwise to reduce them all.

John amends his profit-and-loss forecast, and his cash-flow forecast, as shown in Tables C and D. Table C shows profits only £200 lower, and Table D shows reduced borrowing from month 7. The year-end overdraft falls to £23,250, nearly £19,000 less than his first forecast. The overdraft increases in month 13 but is still nearly £18,000 less than the original forecast.

The new forecasts, like the old ones, do not provide for interest on borrowing, or for John's personal drawings. Neither answers the question: 'When can you repay the loan?' which the lenders are sure to ask. John extends the forecast to month 24, assuming no change in purchases and sales, wages, overheads and ignoring inflation. He realises that this is very rough and ready and unrealistic. But showing the cash-flow in credit for the last few months, he has a pointer to the sort of term he will need for his borrowing, that is 3–5 years rather than 15–20 years.

John believes that the new forecasts can serve as a basis for a preliminary talk with the bank manager. They will then have to be worked on, probably with professional help, before being presented to the bank or to other possible lenders. John will need clearly to set out the assumptions behind any estimated figures in the cash-flow forecast.

Getting realistic forecasts

You may be surprised when you discover how much money you will need as working capital, so don't underestimate your requirements. Many businesses run out of money because they expand too rapidly; this is called overtrading.

An estimated profit margin may appear ample, but total profits may fail to cover outgoings if the volume of sales turns out to be lower than the forecast. Nearly every first attempt at a first profit-and-loss forecast is too ambitious. That is why a cash-flow forecast is needed as it can show when resources are not equal to ambitions. It is easy to recast figures at the business-plan stage to get satisfactory and realistic forecasts to put to a bank or other lender. But look critically at both your original and new assumptions to see whether you are introducing too much wishful thinking.

You should have a picture in your mind of what stage you intend to have reached in one year's or two years' time, even if you cannot make anything other than a very approximate forecast about this. It's important to have a forward plan, against which you can monitor progress. You will be able to take the necessary action if things are not going according to plan.

Chapter 4

Sole trader, partnership, company or co-operative?

Deciding how to trade should be an integral part of your plans, and is something that you should discuss with your professional adviser. There are various considerations and some that might be significant for your business could be quite unimportant for another. The Lawyers For Your Business★ scheme provides a free half-hour consultation with a participating solicitor. They could well help you to decide whether to trade as a:

- sole trader
- partnership
- limited company
- co-operative.

You should periodically review your choice as you can usually change to another legal entity later, as your business develops. Moving from sole trader or partnership to a company doesn't have too many tax snags but switching the other way can be more complicated.

Your choice will affect the tax you pay. Compare your trading position as sole trader or partner with that as a shareholder-owner and salaried director of a limited company. Work through the figures for various options or get an accountant to do so. You have to decide what aspects of taxation are most important for you.

- The rate of corporation tax now payable by small companies is below the basic rate of income tax payable by sole traders.
- Many businesses make losses in their early years. A company's losses can be carried forward and set against profits in future years (or the previous year), while a sole trader or partner may also be able to set losses against other income and gains in the same tax year or against tax paid in up to three earlier years.

- A company director's remuneration need not be fixed until the results of the year's trading are known. This allows you to choose the mixture of salary, dividends and pension that achieves a reasonable balance between minimising the company's corporation tax and the directors' personal tax, taking into account their personal tax allowances and any other income. By contrast, all the profits received by a sole trader or partner are taxed as their personal income.

- A company must pay employer's Class 1 National Insurance contribution on directors' and other employees' salaries in addition to deducting employees' Class 1 contribution from their pay. However, there is no National Insurance on money paid out as dividends. By contrast, a sole trader pays self-employed Class 4 National Insurance on all profits above a certain level (plus a small, flat-rate Class 2 contribution) and builds up entitlement to fewer state benefits than employees.

Tax is not the only consideration. Being a sole trader is relatively simple, but operating as a company offers the protection of limited liability. You should consider the liability of the directors if things go wrong; how to get your money out of the business when you sell up or retire; and the higher costs of complying with the Companies Acts compared with setting up as a sole trader. You may also find it easier to raise large amounts of capital finance if you set up a company.

The Federation of Small Businesses★ publishes *Self-employed or Limited Company?* a useful introductory guide to some of the factors to take into account.

Sole trader

Being a sole trader does not mean you have to work alone. You can, for example, employ others to work in the business. As a sole trader, however, you are entirely responsible for the business: you take all the profits but you are personally liable for all the debts, too. Your personal possessions, home and investments could be at stake if there is not enough money to meet the debts of the business. Many small businesses start as sole traders and are later turned into limited companies. You must tell the Inland Revenue that you are a sole trader, within three months of the last day of the month in which you start self-employment.

Sole traders and partnerships (see below) may trade under their own name or names, or under another name or title. However, if the name that you have chosen to trade under is not your own surname(s), you must indicate the name(s) of the owner(s) on all stationery, and display them in your shop or office or place of work.

Partnership

A business partnership is an association of two or more people trading together as one firm and sharing the profits. The partners are normally *jointly and severally* liable for the whole of the firm's debts, to the full extent of their personal means as if they were sole traders. If one partner should abscond, the others have to pay all the outstanding debts including the absconder's share. An exception to the normal joint and several rule for debts applies to tax (but not VAT).

The partnership as a whole gets a tax return, but the partners must each enter their own share of pre-tax profit on their own tax return and are responsible for paying only their own tax in the same way as if they were sole traders.

A limited partnership can be set up with each partner's liability limited to the amount of capital contributed. But limited partnerships must have at least one partner who is fully liable for the firm's debts and must register with Companies House★ in Cardiff (for England and Wales), Companies House★ in Edinburgh (for Scotland) and the Companies Registry★ in Belfast (for Northern Ireland). Limited partners cannot take part in the management of the business.

Partnerships that go sour can be messy and upsetting, so it is wise to lay down guidelines of who does what and what should happen in the case of a dispute. The resulting agreement should be codified by a solicitor. It should set out:

- the names of the partners
- each partner's share of the profits
- how each partner's share is to be valued if one wants to withdraw from the partnership (e.g., on retirement) or a new partner comes in

- what happens to the share of a partner who dies
- how long the partnership is to run or under what conditions it can be terminated
- how much each partner can draw (e.g., monthly) on account of his or her share of the profit
- how voting rights are divided up
- who signs the cheques
- holiday and sickness arrangements
- what happens if an ex-partner wants to start trading in competition
- whether all the partners must work in the firm or whether one or more may be 'sleeping partners' who just put in money
- any clauses specific to the particular circumstances of the partnership.

Limited liability partnerships

Limited liability partnerships are a form of partnership that came into existence on 6 April 2001. A limited liability partnership is a legal entity separate from its members. The partners' personal wealth will be protected in some circumstances. Limited liability partnerships work much like other partnerships in their structure and the way they are taxed. However, they have many of the characteristics of a limited company and must be registered at Companies House, which can provide free booklets on how they work, the regulations governing them and the registration requirements. Registration entails giving Companies House:

- the partnership's name
- where in UK the partnership is registered
- the registered address of the partnership
- the name, address and date of birth of each partner
- names of partners designated to have certain responsibilities, e.g. for sending the annual accounts to Companies House.

It costs £95 to register a limited liability partnership, £20 to change its name and £35 a year for filing the annual return at Companies House.

Limited company

A limited company is a separate legal entity governed by the rules of company law. The rules require the maintenance of accounts, an annual audit and the disclosure of the company's activities to the general public. Some of the more stringent rules are relaxed for smaller companies.

The shareholder(s) – you can have only one if you want – own the company but are liable for its debts only to the extent of the face value of their shares. However, a director's liability can be extended by personal guarantees given to a bank or other financial institution as security for a business loan. And directors are made personally liable and subject to criminal prosecution if they continue trading or take credit knowing that the company is insolvent or trading in a fraudulent way.

Limited companies may be public or private. If public ('plc'), the shares may be made available to the general public and may be quoted on the Stock Exchange. Private companies – which are the majority – do not offer shares to the public, and style themselves 'Limited' or 'Ltd'.

Setting up a company

Limited companies must be registered with Companies House⋆ in Cardiff (for England and Wales), Companies House⋆ in Edinburgh (for Scotland) and the Companies Registry⋆ in Belfast (for Northern Ireland). All can provide free booklets on how companies work and the rules governing them. Registration entails giving the appropriate Companies House:

- a memorandum of association
- the name of the company and country of registration
- the objects of the company
- a statement of the limited liability of its members
- the amount of share capital and how it is divided into shares
- details of first directors and company secretary including occupation, nationality and a list of other company directorships held within the last five years – a private company can have only one director but this must be a different person from the company secretary
- the address of the company's registered office

- articles of association to cover a variety of internal matters including: the rights and powers of the directors and the members; meetings; votes; issue of new shares; and the restrictions on transfer of shares, such as the right of first refusal for the other members if one of them wishes to dispose of his or her shares
- a statutory declaration that all the formalities have been complied with.

It is often simplest to allow the standard articles of association under the Companies Act to apply, and then list alterations and additions to suit the company's particular circumstances. It costs £20 to register a new company (£80 for a same-day service), £10 for a change of company name (£80 for a same-day service) and £15 a year for filing the company's annual return at Companies House.

Getting professional help

It is important to have professional help in setting up and registering a company. Some lawyers and accountants specialise in this. Also, company registration agents can sell a company off the shelf. The agent has registered the company with stand-in directors, shareholders and secretary, but the company is not operating. You buy the company and your names are substituted for those of the stand-ins. If you buy a ready-made company, you can change its name through Companies House.

Naming and publicising your business

Your choice of trading name must conform to certain rules designed to enable anyone dealing with a business to know the owner's name and address. The owner of a business could trade under his or her surname (if a sole trader) or surnames (if it is a partnership) or full corporate name (if it is a limited company).

But if the business trades under a different name, you must include your surname(s) or corporate name and address on the business stationery. So, for example, if you trade as R. Random, or (Roderick) Random and (Humphrey) Clinker, or Peregrine Pickles Ltd, you are not affected, but formulations such as 'Random's Travel Service', or 'The Perfect Pickle' will require compliance with the disclosure rules. A booklet on business names is available from

Companies House★ in Cardiff (for England and Wales), Companies House★ in Edinburgh (for Scotland) and the Companies Registry★ in Belfast (for Northern Ireland).

Companies and limited liability partnerships must also include on their stationery certain details including the registered name and address and number and place of registration. They must also display the name outside business premises.

Co-operative

A co-operative is a business that is jointly owned by its members and run for their benefit, under a democratic constitution. Generally, everyone has one vote irrespective of the size of his or her investment. Co-operatives come in various forms:

- a worker co-operative, owned and controlled by its employees
- a consumer co-operative, owned and controlled by its customers
- a community co-operative, owned and controlled by the community it serves
- a service or secondary co-operative owned and controlled by the users of the services provided, such as a group of small businesses collectively owning and managing their business premises.

Small co-operatives may involve all the members in day-to-day management matters. Others delegate these powers to an elected committee, which is accountable to the membership. Few worker co-operatives employ a paid manager in the conventional sense of the word, but it is common in other co-operatives.

A co-operative must be commercially viable if it is to survive and compete with other businesses and must be conducted on proper business lines. Members can decide what proportion of the profits should go to reserves and what proportion should be distributed among members. This usually depends on the extent to which they have traded with or taken part in the business of the society.

The principle of co-operation may help to keep the enterprise afloat where ordinary companies would founder. During difficult trading times, for example, members may be willing to reduce their expectations and even make some sacrifices for the good of the whole organisation.

Establishing a co-op

Co-operatives may start in different ways. Many are new businesses, while some are formed by workers or members of the community taking over an existing business: for example, when an existing owner-manager retires and has no family to whom he or she can pass the business on. Selling the business to a workforce that has formed a co-operative can be a viable solution.

A co-operative can be registered with the Financial Services Authority under the Industrial and Provident Societies Act if it has at least three members, with members having limited liability. Alternatively, it could register as a company limited by guarantee, with a minimum of only two members.

Get specialist advice. Many areas of the country are served by a local co-operative development agency or local authority officers with specific responsibility for co-operatives. Alternatively, contact the promoting bodies (see below), which can provide model rules and make registration easier, cheaper and quicker than having a constitution drawn up. They can also provide a tailor-made service on request. Costs can vary between the different agencies and the different legal structures.

Industrial Common Ownership Movement

Industrial Common Ownership Movement (ICOM)* promotes and advises worker co-operatives and other forms of employee ownership. It provides specialist registration and legal services for co-operatives and community enterprises, offers training and consultancy services and publishes guidance booklets. It also provides legal, technical and practical services to its members. Membership is open to all co-operatives, support organisations and sympathisers.

Industrial Common Ownership Finance Limited

Industrial Common Ownership Finance (ICOF)* administers a revolving loan fund on a national basis for co-operative and community enterprises. It too has specific loan funds for particular areas of the country. These are generally from £5,000 to £50,000, for up to 10 years. Enterprises that apply for such loans must be able to demonstrate their co-operative status, and also their commercial viability.

Employee Ownership Scotland

Employee Ownership Scotland (EOS)* offers guidance to groups of people wishing to form employee-owned businesses including co-operatives. Advice covers all forms of business consultancy and arranging finance.

Chapter 5

Buying an existing business

The purchase of an existing business is usually undertaken by people who are already in business and wish to expand their operations or change business venues. But it may make equally sound economic sense for someone starting in business to acquire an established niche in a market. You may want to do this by taking over a going concern, by buying into a company or partnership, by operating a franchise or by organising a management buyout. But if the trade is new to you, be wary. You are unlikely to be able to master it at the same time as learning the complexities of running a business. Bear in mind that you will be competing with people who are already established experts in the field. It is better to get your training and experience first, by working in the trade for a period and attending any relevant training courses.

Taking over a going concern

Find out exactly why the business you are interested in buying is being sold. Typical reasons are that the seller is retiring, in poor health, moving out of the area or to a different type of business. But does the seller know that the business is under some sort of threat and so getting out while the going is good? You may be taking over pending contracts. Has the seller performed them satisfactorily so far? Will you be able to complete them properly and on time?

Can you afford it?

Buying into an existing business generally involves a greater capital outlay than a start-up business, but the right decision means you have a good chance of making a success of the business. However, you may be at risk of overcommitting yourself financially or taking on a business that you do not understand adequately.

When starting a business from scratch, you have time in which to build up your customer base, and your stock level at inception will probably be a moderate one. By contrast, the value of the stock of some types of existing business may be significant, and the business you buy may already have all the up-to-date equipment and fittings you will need.

The contract to buy a business usually stipulates how the price you pay is split between stock, business equipment, goodwill and premises. Get your accountant's advice on this split, which has important implications for income tax when starting in business and for capital gains tax when you eventually sell.

Stock

The contract will state what business stock (also known as stock in trade) is to be sold and on what basis it is to be valued. Valuations are carried out by buyer and seller, or by a professional stock valuer. The basis of valuation should be wholesale value, often determined by reference to its purchase price. Whether or not you are likely to have any use for all the stock once you are running the business, you must expect to have to buy it all.

The value of stock cannot be accurately assessed until completion, so make sure that you have sufficient funds available in case the figure turns out to be a high one. You may be able to persuade the seller to guarantee that the stock will not exceed a certain level, but be careful. You will at once be in difficulty if you do not have sufficient stock when you start trading.

You will also need to finalise arrangements with the seller for stocktaking. Ensure that this is done after the seller has stopped trading and before you start doing so.

Fittings and equipment

The contract will also define the trade fittings and equipment sold with the business. Check that the equipment is well maintained and in good order, with an acceptable working life ahead of it and worth the price being asked. It may be prudent to check all the items of trade fittings and equipment against the schedule immediately before completion of the purchase contract.

Goodwill

A flourishing business may be worth more than the sum of its constituent parts. This is because it benefits from goodwill, an indispensable aspect of a good business. Goodwill is a general designation to cover all the intangible factors that give a business its status and enables it to run profitably. It means different things in different businesses. You as prospective buyer will need to satisfy yourself as far as possible that the goodwill exists and will continue to exist after you take it over. A common-sense approach and a sceptical stance will take you a long way to understanding the essentials of the goodwill in a business, though lack of business experience may hinder your judgement. Professional help should bring to light any serious problems.

In simple terms, goodwill means a good reputation among a strong customer base producing a healthy turnover and profits. The extra value of goodwill may also include figures attributed to items such as leases and fittings for the purposes of accounting and tax. It may also include the personality of the owner. The departure of a popular owner may be followed by a decline in trade. Take a long hard look at yourself. What makes you so special? Can you replace the existing owner without affecting the business adversely? Likewise, particular employees may be vital to the success of the business. Some may be inclined to look for new jobs when a new boss takes over. You will have to make sure of the loyalty of any employees you regard as essential.

The name under which the seller trades may be included in the sale. This may be an important part of the goodwill if you are taking over a flourishing business, but is of no value if you intend to change the name (and thus probably the image) of the business.

How an accountant can help

An accountant's job is to scrutinise the business accounts, both current and going back two or three years. Accounts rarely tell the whole truth but should contain sufficient of the truth to show how the business is structured financially. This will allow your accountant to calculate your financial requirements and to let you know whether you stand a chance of making a go of it. A business from which the proprietor makes a comfortable living but on which there are no outstanding bank loans, for example, may be a potentially lethal trap for the buyer who needs to borrow heavily to buy the business.

An experienced accountant should also be able to judge whether the accounts suggest that the business you wish to buy differs in any important way from similar businesses. But there is no safeguard against a seller who falsifies the accounts, other than perhaps relying on your instinct and that of the people advising you.

How a solicitor can help

A solicitor will advise you on the purchase contract. Both buyer and seller can withdraw from the transaction without being liable for the other's financial outlays before exchange of contracts. After exchange of contracts, both parties are legally committed to the transaction. Any attempt by either one to withdraw risks becoming a costly experience. Avoid signing any document other than the contract (and any related legal documents) provided by your solicitor.

Buying a business can be relatively straightforward if it does not include business premises. Nevertheless, even then you may be safer employing a solicitor. For example, a solicitor can get the necessary agreement from the seller to enter into a non-competition covenant so the seller cannot set up in competition and take the customers. The covenant could prohibit the seller from soliciting the customers of the business and from involvement in any competing business within a defined area for a defined period. The precise terms will depend on the type and location of the business that is being sold.

A solicitor can also draw up other special clauses in the purchase contract: for example, if you need any form of licence (to sell alcohol, for example) or other special permission or approval to enable you to take over the business, the contract may need to provide that the transaction will not be completed if you do not get it.

A solicitor is usually essential if you are buying business premises, whether freehold or leasehold (see Chapter 12), and should be able to advise on whether you need planning permission if you are likely to change the nature of the business in any way.

What to ask the seller

You or your solicitor should make extensive enquiries about the business, to which the seller will probably give many reassuring replies. But the seller is trying to persuade you to buy the business and won't go out of the way to alert you to problems. Indeed, the seller may give information that is misleading or incorrect.

You may have some legal redress against the seller if this happens, but it will be difficult to prove what was said if there is nothing in writing. An experienced solicitor should know the general, all-important queries that need to be raised and should do this in writing and get satisfactory written answers. You must make sure he or she raises points of particular concern to you, to cover areas such as:

- protection of goodwill
- employees of the business – you need a lot of information about them in order to establish what redundancy and other rights they have
- items on lease hire or hire-purchase – the seller cannot sell you these items but you may want to take over existing agreements: business vehicles and cash registers are generally subject to hire-purchase agreements; display freezers are sometimes lent to shop owners; burglar alarms and phone equipment are often leased on medium- to long-term contracts
- continuing contracts with customers to be taken over by the buyer
- planning permission – whether the necessary planning permission for business premises has been obtained and covers work carried out or changes made by the seller
- covenants adversely affecting the property or your ability to carry on a particular type of business from the premises
- covenants applying to a freehold property (possibly set up years ago) and whether they are enforceable – there could be someone waiting to pounce if there is any infringement
- the identity of the landlord if the premises are leasehold, method of paying rent and whether there have been any disputes with the landlord
- whether the landlord's permission is required under the covenants for building work or change of use
- compliance with fire precautions and other safety legislation.

What to ask the local authority

A local authority search provides useful but limited information including nearby road proposals, planning issues, compulsory purchase or demolition orders, liability for road works and financial orders.

The search will not provide information about other property. It won't, for example, tell you if the next-door building is due to be demolished to make way for a supermarket. You can ask for information about planning applications for property in the vicinity, but bear in mind that local authorities have their own guidelines on how much information they will provide.

You are entitled to inspect the planning register at the local authority offices. There you can read the planning history of all properties in the neighbourhood and see what applications are still awaiting a decision. You can also talk to the planning officials about local trends and developments. Look out for pointers to help you assess the future prospects of a business, such as:

- new housing in the neighbourhood – will this bring potential new customers?
- the diversion of a road, or the construction of a bypass – will this adversely affect passing trade or your accessibility to your customers?
- the creation of a pedestrian precinct, which tends to boost trade for shops within the precinct – might it draw trade away from businesses outside it?

Buying a whole company

A seller who runs a business in the form of a limited company may want to pass it on in the same form: not as just a business but as a company. You would buy all the issued shares and would become the owner of the company and have yourself appointed director.

This is different from buying a business in the form of a sole trader – and it is not to your advantage. When you purchase a business in the form of a sole trader, it then has a new and different owner (you), and any problems from past years – with taxation or money claims, for example – will still be the seller's problems. You will probably be able to ignore them unless you choose to settle them, in order to enhance the business's goodwill and reputation.

But if you acquire the business as a company, it still has the same owner – the company – and you inherit all past and any prospective problems. This could involve you in considerable expenditure of time and money, and prevent you from starting with a clean slate.

The apparently simple matter of transferring shares may be supported by a long complicated contract, which contains a great many warranties and indemnities to protect the buyer. But they will be worth nothing if the seller is later found no longer to have any money.

It may be preferable to buy a business without buying the company – doing so either as a sole trade or in the name of your own company. The seller would retain the original company. If he or she refuses, you will have to decide whether to take the risk or let the deal fall through.

Buying into a company

A seller of a limited company may want to sell only a portion of the shareholding. Care should be exercised if you are considering taking this route. The previous owner's continuing involvement (financial and managerial) in the business may safeguard the prosperity of the company but you need to be certain that your business ideas agree. If one of several shareholders in a private company wants to offload a shareholding, the approval of the sale by the company directors may be crucial. They are likely to have the right to veto any sale by refusing to register a transfer of shares.

The value of a whole company may be relatively easy to determine, although there are differing accounting conventions for doing so. But the value of a partial shareholding, particularly a minority shareholding, can be difficult to assess when you buy. You also have to look ahead and consider the price you'll get when you eventually sell, especially if there are restrictions on a shareholder's ability to do so. If the other shareholders are the only available market, you may have either to accede to their price or else to hang on to your shares – a dilemma that arises all too frequently.

These problems can be circumvented by agreement between the shareholders, but take legal advice before committing yourself.

Buying into a partnership

Becoming a partner in an existing business is very different from becoming a shareholder in an existing limited company. Your legal liabilities to the outside world start only from the moment you become a partner. By contrast, in purchasing a company's shares you are buying the company's ongoing obligations as well as its assets. And while buying shares necessarily implies a stake in all the company's assets, entering into a partnership does not automatically mean that you will acquire any rights of ownership over the partnership assets.

If you enter into an unlimited partnership you are *jointly and severally* liable for any debts of the partnership: you are liable for your partner's share of debts as well as your own. Ensure as far as you are able that prospective partners are trustworthy and have sufficient assets to cover their likely share of any debts.

It is important to enter into a written agreement with the existing partners covering at least such essential issues as profit sharing and ownership of the firm's assets. These issues are often not clear-cut. In the long run, unresolved ambiguity and uncertainty can lead to conflict.

Operating a franchise

A company can expand by setting up its own branches. Alternatively, it can become a franchisor and sells its experience and reputation to individuals – the franchisees.

A vast array of franchises is for sale – from fast-food outlets to service industries. The purchase of a franchise enables you to use a particular method to run a particular kind of business and sometimes the right to use and trade under a household name. It also allows you to run your own business and still be part of a large network. You are buying expertise and an image, but the entry price can be high so you must assess whether the potential rewards justify the costs.

A profitable franchise combines a successful business idea with a proper level of support and promotion from the franchisor. The price you pay may give you the exclusive right to distribute goods or offer a certain service within a given area but with no back-up. Decide whether you could set up a similar operation yourself and perhaps save a great deal of money.

You will need to vet thoroughly any prospective franchisor but must expect to be vetted yourself. The better the franchisor, the more concerned they are likely to be that only good-quality franchisees are taken on. You will need to make a good impression.

Banks often have specialised departments to deal with franchises and may be able to offer advice. They also know that buying a suitable franchise helps to minimise the risks of a start-up business. You will need to make your own capital contribution to the initial costs. Banks will generally expect this to be at least 30 per cent of the total, but raising the finance is likely to be easier than in starting a business from scratch.

How franchises work

The diversity of franchised businesses gives rise to various systems. At the core of any franchise agreement is an operations manual covering the essential business techniques that you, the franchisee, are obliged to use. The operations manual is a confidential document and its contents must not be revealed.

When considering whether to take on a franchise, you should bear the following points in mind.

- Becoming a franchisee often means that you will own the business assets such as premises, equipment and so on – although some franchisors prefer to own the business premises and lease them to franchisees.
- You will not own the business method.
- You can usually decide whether you want to trade as a sole trader, in partnership or through a limited company.
- Your trading accounts will be subject to scrutiny and controls set by the franchisor, who may stipulate exactly what accounting systems you are to use. Uniformity among franchisees makes it easier for the franchisor to inspect the accounts and draw management information from them.
- The franchisor will monitor the way you operate the business. The franchisor may stipulate opening hours and retain control

over the décor and furnishings and training of staff. The particular methods and techniques of, for example, preparing and cooking the food in a fast-food chain may be laid down. You may be obliged to buy certain foodstuffs and ingredients only from the franchisor.

- There will generally be strict reporting procedures between you and the franchisor.
- You normally buy the right to trade for only a limited period, typically five years. This may be coupled with the right to renew the franchise at the end of that period.
- The cost to you will be the payment of a capital sum on entering into the agreement and probably regular service fees – possibly based on turnover or profits – while the agreement lasts.

Choosing a franchisor

The service fee that a franchisor charges varies greatly and this may affect your choice of franchise – 10 per cent of turnover being an average amount. Some franchisors, however, may set a somewhat higher rate in return for providing special facilities. Anything grossly excessive should be regarded with suspicion unless there's a demonstrably high level of support to justify it. Cowboy franchisors, for example, might charge an excessively high franchise fee as well as management service fee, which will give you little room for profit. Alternatively, they may charge a fee but offer little or no training or equipment. If their fee is relatively low you may get virtually nothing back.

To protect yourself when considering a franchisor, always seek satisfactory answers to the following questions.

- Is the franchisor a member of the British Franchise Association (BFA)★? If not, why not? BFA members are bound by a code of ethics designed to protect franchisees. The BFA publishes a *Franchisee Guide*.
- What are the experiences of other franchisees? A reputable franchisor cannot have grounds to refuse a request for a list of its franchisees.
- If the business idea is such a money-spinner, why is the franchisor not running the business – or is it the sale of the franchise that is the true money-spinner?

What to look for in a franchise agreement

Always have the franchise agreement thoroughly vetted by your solicitor, and the financial side checked by your accountant. Ensure that the agreement deals with the following questions to your satisfaction.

- Does the initial training provided by the franchisor give you the skills to run the business efficiently?
- What back-up is the franchisor obliged to provide by way of advertising and general promotion, advice and trouble-shooting in return for the service fees you pay?
- What goods and provisions are you obliged to buy through the franchisor? What controls are there over the price the franchisor can charge?
- Do you have exclusive trading rights in a defined geographical area? This is generally regarded as one of the key elements of a franchise.
- How long does the franchise run for? On what terms can you renew it?
- Are there any restrictions on your business activities when the franchise ends?
- Is the continuation of the franchise dependent on a minimum level of turnover or profit or any other factors? It would be disastrous if the franchise could be withdrawn without compensation after you have paid a large sum to buy it
- What will happen if you want or are obliged to sell the business or if you die? The better franchisors want control over the vetting of any new franchisee. Your ability to sell the business as a going concern may depend on the franchisor's goodwill and/or the quality of the prospective buyer. Is the franchisor obliged to buy the business from you if no other satisfactory franchisee can be found?

Most franchisors use standard forms of franchise agreement in order to maintain uniformity in business operations. Your ability to negotiate on terms you don't like may be limited.

Buying a business from an employer

Employees occasionally have the opportunity to buy the business in which they work – possibly through a management buy-out. Before doing so, you should carefully scrutinise the owner's motives for selling and of course the accounts of the business.

If you are planning to buy a business that has failed, you will not find it easy to raise the necessary finance unless you know exactly why the original company went out of business and have convincing proposals for putting things right.

If you have been made redundant by the winding-up of a company or know of a company that has been wound up, consider whether there is any part of the operation or assets (some of the workshop plant, for example) that you could buy and use in starting a project of your own.

There is little to stop employees who leave an existing company from setting up in competition. Even if there is a clause in their contract of employment restricting their future business ventures, the courts will not uphold a contract that is a restraint of trade and denies anyone the right to earn a living. However, the ex-employer may stop former employees from making use of trade secrets or confidential information by taking out an injunction.

Chapter 6

Marketing and selling

The success of your business depends on how you market and sell your product or service. The two terms are not interchangeable. Marketing covers everything from market research, product planning and product development to product promotion by, for example, advertising. Selling is the process of negotiating and carrying out that transaction.

Marketing and selling are continuous processes. You should always be looking ahead and planning your strategy for the coming months and years. The time to start planning for sales is when your product or service is still on the drawing board. At this point, nothing is lost if you discover that your idea will not command a large enough market to make a profit.

You should begin your marketing strategy by asking yourself some questions.

What can you offer customers?

What do you have to sell? If it is something produced by other people, for which you are going to act as wholesaler, retailer, agent or dealer, you probably have no influence on the actual form of the product. The choice is between one brand and another, between the cheap and popular or the expensive and exclusive varieties of the product.

Refining your product

If you are going to sell something you have designed (or had designed for you) and intend to produce, you may decide to produce it in several versions, with varying functions and at different price levels. Do not stick inflexibly to your original idea if there's a high risk it won't work. Be prepared to scrap it if necessary.

Your product may be more sophisticated than the prospective buyers are likely to want. It may be too expensive for the ultimate consumer or there may not be enough customers to buy it at the price you need to charge. You may have to look for ways to reduce expensive labour-intensive processes, for example, or use cheaper materials. You may have to modify the product to give it more retail appeal or decide to find another market for it, or produce two varieties for different types of user. A simpler version may initially sell better and pave the way for a more sophisticated one incorporating new features in response to the first customers' reactions. You may decide to make a range of related products.

Meeting the demand

The product may require the skills of several craftspeople: for example cabinet-makers and precision engineers. Make sure from the start that you will have a supply of skilled labour to depend on. It is no use building up a market for a product if you cannot guarantee its supply. It might be better to design something that can be made by less skilled labour.

Ask yourself if the demand for your product is likely to be seasonal. A new super-efficient nutcracker, for example, is likely to sell readily only in the period before Christmas. You may need other products to keep your plant and labour occupied for the rest of the year.

Defining your service

Where you are quite simply selling a service plus your expertise, the need to define it precisely applies just as much as to a product. If, for example, you are setting up a security business, you should decide whether you can supply a delivery service complete with armoured cars, or human guards, or guard dogs, or specialist advice on how people can improve the security of their home or factory.

In the case of an agency or consultancy, define your scope as closely as possible. Rather than grandly planning to become an import-export agent, aim to trade with particular geographical areas and in specific products – preferably ones you are already familiar with. You are more likely to succeed as a consultant if you limit your field to where your particular expertise lies. Do not wait for your clients' reactions to tell you on what topics you are not qualified to give advice.

Where will you find customers?

The nature of the product or service will give a general idea of your likely customer base. Woollen sweaters are for most people; accountancy software is most likely to be bought by businesses; easy-to-install damp-proof window frames could interest the building industry and the d-i-y enthusiast. A solar-panel water-heating system may still have a limited market in Britain, but could be the basis of an export trade until the domestic market develops.

Work out the best way to sell your products to your prospective customers, whether through a retail shop or a department store, through a wholesaler, the Internet or by mail order, through agents or directly, in the UK or abroad.

Public reference libraries

You can do a lot of market research from sources ready to hand, starting with a public reference library. It should have a commercial section with trade directories; publications such as *Yellow Pages* and phone books covering the whole country; directories of foreign importers; official digests of statistics; and much more. Some libraries offer research services, for a fee.

Academic libraries

In any university, school of business studies or similar establishment where economics, management studies or business studies are taught, you should find not only an invaluable library but also experts to consult – even students willing to do your market research for you for a modest fee.

The Internet

The Internet is another useful source of information. Type in some keywords on a search engine such as Google (www.google.co.uk) to see what is thrown up and where it might lead.

Government statistics

The Office for National Statistics (ONS)★ can provide a vast amount of information, some of which may be helpful in working out where your market might be. Its free catalogue *The Source* lists the kinds of facts and figures available and relevant to business: for example, on industrial production, financial services, the retail trade and external trade. Much of this is published in a series called *Product Sales and Trade Data*.

Someone planning a comprehensive marketing strategy may want to study figures relating to national income and expenditure and population trends and projections. This might give you an idea of what proportion of what kind of people (teenagers, pensioners, etc.) is likely to want your product.

Some publications with useful facts and figures include *UK Directory of Manufacturing Businesses*; *Population Trends* (quarterly); *Family Spending* (annual); *Overseas Trade Statistics of the United Kingdom* (monthly); and *UK Service Sector: Retail Sales* (monthly). Ask for them at a public reference library as they are rather expensive to buy.

Trade organisations, trade journals, trade exhibitions

As you are a novice, you should snatch at every opportunity of consulting those who are already experts; your trade association should be able to help you. This will be listed in the *Directory of British Trade Associations* (available in public reference libraries). If your product is to be sold to some trade or industry, you can use its trade directories to compile a list of potential customers.

Trade journals can inform you about the prospects of your trade, future developments and new products, and will give you an idea of who your potential buyers might be. You may find details of journals and publications by looking at *BRAD's Media Lists*, which are categorised by subject.

Trade exhibitions can do a similar job, so check the *Financial Times* regularly as it publishes the dates and venues of forthcoming trade exhibitions. So does the *Exhibition Bulletin,*★ which offers the information worldwide and two years or more in advance, making planning ahead easier.

Test-marketing

If you have started to manufacture your product in your spare time and are wondering whether to go into full production, try to test your market. This can be done for a small outlay, perhaps by distributing a few hundred leaflets or putting a couple of dozen cards in shop windows. Do not distribute too many leaflets at a time, in case you would then not be able to deal with the number of requests.

Space out the distribution. This should give you some idea of whether anyone in the district is interested in what you have to offer.

Who are your competitors?

Yellow Pages will list similar businesses in your area, so if you are counting on local trade you can make yourself familiar with your competitors' products. Watch particularly for competitors' publicity and advertising: yours will have to be different and better. Send for their promotional literature and price lists, and attend trade exhibitions to see what they offer.

If yours is a service industry, try approaching a similar firm for advice. You may find one operating in another area that is willing to show you round the premises and answer questions. But do not expect your local firms to welcome and train more competition. Do not give your ideas away to someone who may beat you to it.

If a competitor's product is sold through retail outlets, go and view it at the point of sale to discover how it is displayed and promoted. Your objective should be to find out how your product would compare. Why should people prefer it to any other? Has it any unique features? What special qualities have other products got that could be incorporated in your own product if copyright or patents don't prevent you from copying?

What will you charge your customers?

The price you ask for a product or service can be arrived at in various ways, and largely depends on your costs, competition, demand and the going rate.

Costs
At the very least, you want a price made up of the cost of manufacture (labour, materials, overheads) plus a percentage mark-up for profit. You must allow for discounts for quantity orders or for quick payment (for example, in seven days) and for anything else that might encourage greater purchase or quicker settlement. If you sell to another firm, you will probably need to offer credit because your competitors may do so. You must cost this in, for example by including the extra expense of your own overdraft.

If you sell through a wholesaler you must allow for the wholesaler's and retailer's profit as well as your own plus VAT if applicable while settling on the price to the ultimate customer. If you do not include all these elements, you may price yourself out of the market.

Competition

Competitors may be able to produce an item for a lower cost or may manufacture more of them while accepting a lower profit margin. You should identify your competitors and find out what they offer at what prices. For most products there are several price ranges, and manufacturers tailor their goods to fit into one of these. Some offer several product ranges, each one for a different category. Cosmetics, for example, tend to be cheap and cheerful for the young, medium priced for the average user, and extremely expensive for the wealthier consumer. You should decide at an early stage into which price category your product will slot.

If your costs are too high for the lower or middle price range, you will have to aim at the higher price market. In this case, you'll have to persuade customers that your product contains some special or unique quality. There are some categories of goods where a high price can be a selling point: it can reassure customers that an item is at the luxury, quality or exclusive end of the spectrum. It can be a psychological error to charge less.

Demand

Demand and what customers are prepared to pay will set an upper limit on what you can charge. If you produce a range of related goods, some will be more wanted than others. Your pricing should be based on a profit margin averaged out over the whole range. You may try loss-leader pricing of one or more items, selling at cost or very little above it. This may stimulate sales and act as bait to capture a large share of the market quickly. But you will be the loser if you sell all the low-profit items and none of the high-profit ones.

The going rate

Pricing based on the going rate incorporates the elements of competition and demand. There is usually a recognised going rate in service industries. You would need to offer something extra to charge more: for example, being on call at all hours or offering a particularly comprehensive or fast service. Where there is no going rate, you must cost your own time carefully when calculating your overheads.

Promoting your product

Once you have settled on a price for your goods you then need to decide the best way or ways of attracting the attention of your potential customers. Your ideas are also likely to be affected by the wide disparity in costs between using the media, for example, or direct-mail advertising.

The media

Which of the various media you use to advertise in will depend very much on the nature of your product or service, and how much you can afford. There are plenty of small local advertising agencies whose names can be found in *Yellow Pages* or from the Institute of Practitioners in Advertising (IPA).★ What you will be paying for is know-how: an agency should be able to design your advertising, advise on its content and wording, and place it in the appropriate medium – including possibly radio and TV – at the right times. Always ask to see specimens of work and get an estimate before you engage an agency.

Local press

The local press is particularly suited to a service or business that relies on local customers: for example, plumber, electrician, hair-dresser, launderette, florist. The cheapest advertisement is an insert in the classified advertisement section. This does not catch the eye but waits for someone looking for that type of service or product, so to be effective it should appear regularly. If you want to catch the reader's passing glance, a display advertisement will be more suitable or, if your budget permits, a larger, specially designed adver-tisement on an editorial page. You could include a Freepost coupon. To be most effective, it should be placed on the outside edge of the page, where it is easy to cut out. Such an advertisement, too, should appear regularly.

Many local papers will design a display advertisement but a professionally designed one is likely to be more eye-catching. You can find a graphic designer through *Yellow Pages*, but check the cost before commissioning the advertisement.

Another way to reach local markets is to pay a newsagent to slip a leaflet inside every newspaper delivered.

National press

Advertising in national newspapers and magazines is suited to a firm hoping to sell by mail order. It is essential to choose publications that are right for the type of goods – women's clothing in women's pages and magazines, sets of spanners in d-i-y magazines. Use the trade press if your customers are other businesses rather than the general public.

Press releases

Use a press release to tell the local, national or trade press – and radio and TV – about special events, such as the opening of a new workshop or the launch of a new product. To have the best chance of getting anything published, find the person in charge of the relevant section of a newspaper or whatever and send a suitably written press release that could form the basis of a small article or feature.

Editors and journalists don't necessarily spend a lot of time hunting down good news stories or ideas for features. They often respond to what comes to them. Start reading newspapers and magazines critically to get an idea of what they are looking for. Ask yourself how certain companies or products manage to get a mention.

A paragraph or two of editorial copy can be more effective than any advertisement. Include all relevant details in the press release – your name and address, the price of the product and how people can buy it. If you can't find a news angle, look for a human-interest angle with the hope of getting in the features pages of the papers. The better written and more concise the press release, the more likely it is to get in. A good picture may increase the chances of inclusion. If you place an advertisement at the same time, you may get an editorial mention – but the two are not invariably linked.

The services of a public relations firm (use *Yellow Pages*) may help in getting the best out of free publicity.

Trade exhibitions

Trade exhibitions and local trade fairs have a triple function: market research; finding out what your competitors are producing; and selling your own goods to firms. They are not usually open to the general public. The trade press will tell you where and when appropriate exhibitions are taking place and how to book space. There may be several suitable ones each year.

Exhibitions can be expensive. You have to hire the stand and arrange for someone competent to be there to explain and perhaps demonstrate the product, distribute literature and note down enquiries (to be scrupulously followed up). The exhibition should at least earn back its expenses eventually. Do not rush in without thought and preparation.

You may not be able to afford a stand or your range of goods may not justify a separate stand. See whether you can find firms selling related products that may be willing to share a stand. The chamber of commerce, a small business club or the exhibition's promoter may be able to suggest suitable firms.

You are more likely to attract potential buyers' attention if you write to them beforehand, preferably by name. Try to find out the relevant person to contact by phoning a firm first. Send your promotional literature and the number of your stand and invite them to have a chat with you.

Direct mail advertising

Distributing leaflets through a few hundred neighbourhood doors is the simplest form of direct mail. If you want to cover larger or more distant areas, you will have to entrust the work to a specialist firm: look in *Yellow Pages* under 'Circular & Sample Distributors'. The Royal Mail's Door-to-Door service can deliver your advertising, normally on the regular postal rounds. The charge is based on the weight of the material: there are five weight categories, with a 100g maximum. The more you send, the lower the rates (but there is a £500 minimum charge).

Alternatively, you may want to target customers directly by name. To do this, you should send out a sales letter, accompanied by a leaflet, brochure or catalogue. The promotional literature must be eye-catching, and designed by a professional if possible. Mailsort offers a range of discount services for pre-sorted mail, which apply to bulk mailings of 4,000 or more letters or 1,000 or more packets. You must have them sorted in advance by postcode. These services are unlikely to prove useful until your business has expanded greatly.

Business Reply and Freepost are two of the services offered by Royal Mail to direct mail advertisers. With Business Reply, you send out, for your customers' replies, a postcard or envelope printed with your address and needing no stamp: first and second class options are available. With Freepost, customers can use either pre-printed cards or envelopes provided by you or use their own stationery. No stamp is needed if the word 'Freepost' is added to the address. You pay the postage, a small handling charge on each reply you receive and an annual licence fee. Details of these and other services and publications on the effective use of direct mail can be obtained from Royal Mail Sales Centres.*

Mailing lists

If you want to sell to other businesses, you can make up your own mailing list out of entries in the trade directories. Although relatively inexpensive, this is laborious as it is more effective if you address the letter individually to a firm's buyer. You may get the relevant person from a trade reference book, a trade association or by phoning the firm. A good word-processing computer package should be able to handle this. For advertising to local firms, use relevant names and addresses from *Yellow Pages* in the same way.

For advertising to individual consumers, you can try to make up your own mailing list from the electoral register. Alternatively, many organisations have subscription or membership lists they are prepared to sell. Some will exchange lists. Two organisations use each other's lists – but you, as a beginner, will not have anything to swap. More commonly, organisations will rent lists. If a list is large, you may be able to rent part of it so that you can test how well the list works for your purposes. Do not be too surprised if the part that you are offered for the test turns out to be the best part of the list. To get a more realistic idea of how useful the list is going to be to you, ask for a cross-section – say, one out of every six names. A large percentage of any full list is likely to be undeliverable – 'no such address' or 'gone away'.

An organisation may insist on vetting the offer you intend to send by direct mail as well as the use of a specialist mailing company to do the addressing and posting, to prevent you from copying the list.

You will get the names and addresses of those who reply, and these become part of your own list, which you later may sell, rent out or exchange. List brokers may be able to help you find lists, for a fee. Look for brokers who are members of the Direct Marketing Association.* They should meet certain standards concerning how, for example, the list is compiled.

Response rates and costs

Calculate the likely postage cost before sending any direct mail. It may cost you 27p for each letter sent, but the cost becomes £27 for each reply if you send out 10,000 letters and the response rate is 1 per cent. The response rate to direct mail advertising is variable, depending on the product, the market and the care taken in preparation. A response of between 3 and 5 per cent should be considered as extremely good. But responses don't all result in orders. After your first mailshot you should be able to calculate whether the resulting business has earned back its promotion costs plus some profit.

Mailing Preference Service

The use of direct mail is an effective form of advertising that must be used with care. Many people resent receiving mail addressed to them from a company with which they have had no dealings and of which they may not have heard. They may just bin it unopened or even send it back for you to pick up the cost of postage.

It is in your interests to subscribe to the Mailing Preference Service (MPS).* The MPS gives subscribers a quarterly listing of people who have positively requested that they should not be sent any direct mail advertising. It also makes available a list of those people who have asked to be sent more details of goods available in some particular category. If you do your mailing through a list broker or a mailing house, make sure that it uses an MPS list.

Data protection

Data protection laws apply to information ('personal data') about identifiable living individuals. They cover not only sensitive information but also names, addresses and phone numbers even though they may already be in the public domain in directories and so on. They apply to data on computers and in paper filing systems.

People using personal data – known as data controllers – may have to notify the Office of the Information Commissioner. You may need to notify if you control the data in some way, even if it is held by an agency. It is an offence not to notify when required or to use your data in a way that is not in accordance with your register entry. The current notification fee is £35 for one year. Even if you do not actually need to notify, you still need to comply with the principles. Data must be:

- processed fairly and lawfully
- processed for limited purposes
- adequate, relevant and not excessive
- accurate
- kept no longer than necessary
- processed in accordance with the data subject's rights
- secure
- not transferred to countries without adequate protection.

The data register is open to public inspection. Any individual about whom data is stored is entitled to a copy of the data (for a small fee), a description of the reason for which the data is used, a note of the potential recipients, and (except in limited circumstances) information on the source of the data. Individuals have a right to opt out of having their data used for direct marketing. You may need their explicit consent before using more sensitive data. People have the right to claim compensation for damage and for distress, in some circumstances, if these rights are breached.

Trade associations, your local Business Link★ (or the alternatives outside England) and other business organisations can advise on how data protection laws affect your business. The Office of the Information Commissioner can supply full information and application forms. You should ask your accountant to add data protection to the checklist for your business to make sure that you operate correctly and/or notify the Information Commissioner as required.

Selling

How successful you are in getting orders will depend on your selling technique.

- Appear confident about calling on firms to buy your product or service. Selling is a key part of any business. Be prepared to develop a thick skin.
- Display a detailed knowledge of your product or service, a readiness to explain it fluently and possibly to give a demonstration. Don't sell aggressively.
- Listen carefully to your potential customers. Show an obvious interest in what they want. Understand their business and be able to discuss it intelligently.
- Keep to yourself the fact that you personally happen to use a product or service of the potential buyer's competitor.
- Present the right appearance. This might be crucial for services such as consultancy, since you may have nothing else to show your client.
- Add value to the sale by offering, e.g., a service – installation, spare parts and servicing – alongside your product, especially if you are hoping for repeat custom. Find a sub-contractor that can provide the service.

Maintain records of your customers, how much they buy and when – a computer database could prove useful. Ask them if they are satisfied. Treat complaints in a friendly spirit and put right anything that needs rectifying. Keep in regular touch, so that you are in the forefront of their minds when they think of buying.

Selling to shops

At the most basic level, this is a question of taking round a sample of your product to appropriate shops in the district and persuading them to stock it.

- Make an appointment to see the shop's owner or manager. Do not simply turn up unannounced at the busiest time.

- Make yourself familiar with competing products, their prices and their drawbacks. Point out the advantages of your products without obvious criticism of rival products.
- Be clear about the price of your product, but be willing to allow the retailer an attractive discount.
- Decide in advance whether to offer a sale-or-return deal: it is better not to. But if one particular product does not sell well, you could offer to buy it back in order to get the shop to take more of the merchandise that does sell.
- Be prepared to prove that you can guarantee supplies and will stick to delivery dates.
- Have the product or range of your products packaged as it will look when displayed in a shop window or on a shelf.
- Sometimes it helps to offer a small display aid, to show your product to its best advantage. Make clear to the shop owner that this is on loan to display your product, not a gift nor for use to show off someone else's goods.

When you sell to larger shops and chain stores you should make an appointment with the appropriate buyer. The *Retail Directory* (from a reference library) gives some names; find out others by phoning.

- Pay particular attention to the presentation of your product.
- Know your maximum capacity and the size of orders you can guarantee to deliver and your most dependable delivery dates.
- Be prepared to prove that you can finance your increased output.
- Leave some room for negotiating when it comes to discussing price.
- Most large companies pay invoices on their first accounting day after 30 days have passed from receipt of the invoice – this is good reason to invoice customers promptly and correctly, offering no excuse for further delaying payment. Ask for staged payments on a big contract: for example, part payment with the order and then percentage payments at various stages of production or delivery. For more on getting paid, see Chapter 16.

Employing an agent

You may prefer to concentrate on the production side and get someone else to sell for you, especially if you have no time or talent for selling. You could use an agent who knows and is known in the business, who has the necessary contacts and who can keep you up-to-date on what the competition is doing. Your agent will need to be primed with any necessary technical information and supplied with promotional literature, possibly backed up with advertising.

The agent's commission will reduce your profit margin, but perhaps you would not have a profit without an agent. An agent usually represents more than one firm. You can never guarantee that the agent is trying as hard for you as for the others. An agent will work hardest for products offering the highest return.

Look for an agent in the trade press, trade directories, *Yellow Pages* (under 'Manufacturers' Agents' and 'Marketing & Advertising Consultants') or advertise for one. Negotiate an agreement that ensures both parties are clear about the terms.

Mail-order selling

Direct-response mail-order selling is a system in which advertise-ments invite customers to order goods to be sent to them directly. It is usual to offer a no-quibble money-back guarantee if the customer does not want the goods after inspecting them. Most of the relevant codes of practice require this.

Payment is usually by cheque with order or by debit or credit card. Your bank's business banking centre should be able to give advice on how to set up this facility. There will be a service charge or commission of up to 5 per cent which you will have to build into your costs and pricing. Some firms offer credit terms, but these are usually catalogue mail-order houses rather than firms selling their own products.

Products suitable for mail-order selling should fall into one or more of the following descriptions.

- They should be light in weight and strong enough not to break in transit, or bulky but capable of being compactly and securely packed (e.g., many types of garden sheds and greenhouses are sold by mail order).
- They are aimed at a market where the convenience of buying by post or phone outweighs the disadvantage of not being able to see the product before purchase.

- They are in some way new, unique or hard to find, and not obtainable in ordinary retail shops. Examples might be a craft product or something for a minority taste.
- They are available in normal shops but at a much higher price. The price you charge for your product must take into account the advertising costs – often as much as one-third of the selling price; delivery and packing; the cost of replacing damaged articles; and bad debts if you sell on credit. Make sure these costs do not take away the price advantage. Low-priced items may not be worth selling by mail order.

Your customers must be left in no doubt about the total cost of any goods offered, with postage/delivery and packing charges clearly set out if these are added to the basic price.

Your packing, despatch and administration must be up to scratch. Before starting the operation, ensure that you have an efficient system (perhaps on computer) for recording the product sold, the dates of purchase and despatch and the name and address of each customer. You should be confident that you have the stocks and the extra capacity to meet a sudden increase in demand and can deliver within the promised period, typically 30 days. Contact the customer immediately if you can't meet the time limit. Offer a refund or, if the customer agrees, give a firm date for the despatch of the order or fortnightly progress reports.

You must comply with rules designed to protect consumers and maintain confidence. Sources of information on this include the following.

- The Direct Marketing Association★ has a code of practice that is binding on its members.
- The European Distance Selling Directive covers selling by direct mail or over the telephone or Internet. Compliance with its rules is compulsory.
- The Mail Order Protection Scheme (MOPS)★ is run by national newspapers. You'll need approval to advertise in the national newspapers. You must pay a fee to a central fund that indemnifies readers against loss caused by a firm's failure to supply goods ordered if it is liquidated or ceases to trade. If you are approved to join, you must display the MOPS logo in your advertisement. Local papers offer similar schemes.

- The Periodical Publishers Association (PPA)* runs a similar scheme for magazine adverts. The PPA scheme is not centrally run, nor funded by contributions from advertisers. Instead, each individual publisher requires would-be advertisers to complete application forms asking for details of their business. On the basis of this information, a judgement is made as to whether the applicants should be allowed to solicit money off the page in the publications.

- The British Codes of Advertising and Sales Promotion has its own rules. To ensure that your advertisement will be acceptable, contact the Advertising Standards Authority (ASA).* Its Copy Advice Team can give assistance and discuss your proposals. It also has guidelines on direct marketing, including list and database practice.

If you advertise in several newspapers and magazines, it is worth using a simple code to distinguish replies from each source. This tells you which one brings in the most business.

Using the phone

You can use telemarketing to back up a sales promotion or advertising campaign. A telemarketing bureau, for example, could send out product details, handle questions about what you have to offer and even take orders. If you wish to sell in this way, you will almost certainly want to use a specialist telemarketing firm – the Direct Marketing Association* can provide a list of telemarketing bureaux members or look in *Yellow Pages* under 'Telemarketing'. Make sure you choose a firm that is registered with the Telephone and Fax Preference Services.* Such a firm provides lists of people who have requested not to be contacted by telephone or fax. It is an offence to send unsolicited direct-marketing faxes to an individual, though not to a business.

Phone services can also be used to give after-sales' customer care. Failing to offer such a service could put your type of business at a competitive disadvantage. Take this into account when you plan your business and decide whether you can provide an alternative form of customer care.

Dealing with customers by phone needs to be handled sensitively to avoid having the opposite of the desired effect. British Telecom (BT)* publishes a helpful free guide, *Building Relationships*, on this topic.

Using the Internet

Doing business on the Internet – 'e-commerce' – allows you to break into the marketplace without having to develop a physical presence. It can help you reach a widespread specialist market and sell abroad. The Internet can be used for business promotion, as a shop window, an ordering system, a payment system or direct selling. Be realistic, however, about how much impact your e-commerce site will have, as early optimism about how e-commerce would conquer the world was misplaced.

You can set up a website using the templates provided by an Internet service provider or pay for a professional website designer. They are listed in *Yellow Pages* under 'Internet Providers' and 'Internet Services'. A website should have:

- physical contact details (i.e. your company name, address and phone number)
- clear information on things such as costs and delivery times
- a system that confirms the order made over the Net and allows customers to check whether it has been processed
- an explanation of the security measures in use when sending personal details
- a statement on data protection and privacy.

In the UK, websites must conform to the 'legal, decent, honest and truthful' rules of the Advertising Standards Authority (ASA).★ Remember to build into your budget the costs of setting up your site and maintaining it.

You can register your website's presence with the various search-engines. This will enable potential customers to locate you even if they have not heard of you or don't have your web address. Having links to your website from other relevant and well-used sites improves your chances of getting business through the Internet.

A useful place to get information on using the Internet is the Interactive Media in Retail Group (IMRG).★ The IMRG membership includes small web designers through to large information technology vendors. Another organisation that promotes e-commerce is e-centreUK.★ The DTI's UK Online for Business★ website provides information and details of a number of guides.

Chapter 7

Organising your accounts

The figures that your business generates are an index of its health and growth. Maintaining good records is essential for:

- the Inland Revenue
- Customs & Excise, if you register for VAT
- your bank manager, who may require regular information
- your accountant, who charges by the hour, so should not be given lots of untidy bits of paper which take a long time to sort out
- keeping control of your business.

You should keep proper accounts that are summarised at the end of each month, coupled with a stock-take or an estimate of the value of your stock. Find out whether you achieved a profit during the period and whether you have enough money to cover your expenses for the coming month. You don't have to make elaborate calculations. Rough monthly accounts, backed up by an accountant's quarterly report, will enable you to stay in control and anticipate any problems.

It is not good enough to rely solely on the annual accounts, which are not available until the following year is well advanced. By taking a close interest in the monthly figures (or even weekly figures, if appropriate), you can spot problems while there may still be time to put things right and can plan ahead for improvements or expansion if things are going well.

Although you may employ an accountant to point up any problems, you will already have a fair idea of what he or she might find if you have monitored the finances closely, anticipated problems and thought about how to remedy them. Your accountant could undertake the monthly monitoring, but that would involve an extra expense that your new business may not be able to afford. For advice on how to find an accountant, see Chapter 3.

Even if you hand over everything to an accountant, make sure you watch and understand the figures so that you can make sense of the accountant's reports and relate them to your own day-to-day experience.

Keeping business records

Business records may be retained and presented in a variety of ways, depending very much on the type of business for their format. However, one feature is common to all systems: all records must be backed by evidence that the receipts and payments recorded have actually been made. So be sure to file safely all of the following:

- cheque-book stubs
- cancelled cheques – tell the bank to return them to you
- bank paying-in books – use these, not paying-in slips
- bank statements – whether you are a sole trader, partnership or company, it's easier to have separate accounts for business and private life even if they are at the same bank
- copies of your own invoices, receipts and delivery notes
- your suppliers' invoices, receipts and delivery notes
- receipts, wherever possible, for minor purchases made in cash
- copies of all VAT returns
- any other relevant paperwork.

You should also store records of any private money going in and out of the business: for example, a loan from an investor and any money that you draw out to live on. A useful guide is the Inland Revenue leaflet *Self-Assessment: A Guide to Keeping Records for the Self-employed*, available from tax offices (in the phone book under 'Inland Revenue').

No two firms' sets of books are identical, as every business has some individual aspects that must be recorded, and different people have their own notions of which business records require the closest monitoring. Your accountant can set up the books for your particular requirements and teach you how to keep them. A book-keeper may be able to teach a member of your family who can relieve you of the task, until your business needs a full-time book-keeper. You can also teach yourself the elements of book-keeping from one of a variety of books on the subject.

The 'books' you will need

To keep even simple accounts, you may require several 'books'. They need not be paper-based. Computer accounting software for small businesses is widely available, but you must still keep the original paper record of your sales, purchases and other similar transactions. You don't necessarily require all the books listed below: it depends how complicated your business is and what you find useful. You should reconcile all the entries in your cash book with your bank statements.

Cash book

The cash book is the most basic account book to record what goes in and out of your bank account. It records all your payments and receipts and tells you how much ready money you have. Record in columns the date and amount; your cheque number, reference number and name of supplier for payments; the invoice number and name of customer for receipts. Add other columns that are relevant to your business: for example, a miscellaneous column.

Wages book

You must record pay in a wages book if you have employees. Show gross earnings, and deductions for income tax, National Insurance, pension scheme, other deductions, net pay and the employer's National Insurance contributions. You can buy suitable books from a business stationer or appropriate computer software.

Petty cash book

Record in a petty cash book small out-of-pocket expenses paid by you or your staff in the course of work: for example, fares, taxis or the window-cleaner. Pay the money out of a float drawn at intervals from the bank and duly recorded in the cash book (see above) and the purchases book (see below). The petty cash book is like the purchases book, with columns for different types of expenditure. Include VAT details if you are registered for VAT.

Sales and purchases books

If your business is not purely cash because you buy and sell with payment at a later date, you will need a sales day book to record sales invoices as they are sent out as well as a purchases day book to note your purchases of goods and services. The latter should be an analysis book, ruled with a number of vertical columns in which you classify your different kinds of expenditure: materials, direct labour and the various sorts of overheads. If you are working on paper rather than computer, get a book with enough columns. How many columns you will need depends on your particular expenses and on how minutely you want to break down the figures.

By adding up each column every month, you will see exactly how much each of your business expenses came to. The total of these different totals will give you your whole month's costs. If you are registered for VAT, you will need a VAT column in both sales and purchases books, to record the amount of VAT that other people pay you and the VAT that you pay out. You will need this information for your VAT returns.

Ledgers

If your business expands or becomes more complex, you will need to start keeping ledgers.

- The sales ledger is based on the sales day book. It records the individual accounts for customers, showing how much each has bought in any given period and the date of payments. This enables you to keep an eye on slow payers. It helps plan future marketing strategy. It may show, for example, that 80 per cent of your trade is with a few customers placing big orders, 20 per cent with many customers placing small orders. You will then have to decide whether to go on accepting small orders whose costs are high in relation to profits, in the hope that the small customers may be encouraged to grow into bigger ones.
- The purchases ledger is based on the purchases day book, and records transactions with each supplier. It shows the suppliers who get the largest share of your custom. These will be most likely to give credit or better cash discounts.
- The general ledger records impersonal payments including the sale and purchase of equipment, rent and rates, services. It also shows the totals of income and expenditure.

Double-entry book-keeping

Ledgers are the foundation for a double-entry book-keeping system. While a full explanation requires a book to itself, the underlying principle is simple: every transaction is recorded twice, once as a debit and once as a credit, according to whether it is regarded from your point of view as either buyer or a seller.

You should record every purchase as a credit in your suppliers' purchases ledger and a debit to you in the general ledger. When you pay a supplier, note it as a credit in your cash book and a debit for the supplier in the purchases ledger.

Every sale you make should be recorded as a debit in your customers' sales ledger and a credit to you in the general ledger. When a customer pays you, show a debit in the cash book and a credit to you in the sales ledger.

Using your figures

Accurate financial records allow you to make calculations showing how your business is progressing. The all-important one is your monthly net profit. To arrive at this, you need to draw up a monthly trading account and a profit-and-loss account.

Trading account

The monthly trading account will enable you to work out your monthly gross profit. You calculate it by adding up your total sales for the month, and then subtracting the month's labour costs, materials costs and the difference between the value of your opening and closing stocks.

Helen has a full-time job. She has set up a small manufacturing business at the weekend, which she hopes will eventually become her full-time occupation. Her product sells at £20 per unit. Her materials cost £10, labour £2. Using the sales, purchase and labour totals shown by her books, Helen draws up a trading account (see below).

Helen has valued her stock at materials and labour costs only. She also has overheads of £800 a month, which enter the calculation to find the monthly net profit.

Helen's trading account for one month

	£		£
Opening stock		Sales	4,000
(100 units @ £12)	1,200		
Purchases of materials			
(200 @ £10)	2,000		
Labour (200 @ £2)	400		
	3,600		
Less closing stock			
(80 @ £12)	960		
	2,640		
Balance, i.e. gross profit	1,360		
	4,000		4,000

Profit-and-loss account

A profit-and-loss account shows the net profit, and it can be combined with the trading account in a single calculation. There is no special presentation that must be followed. Helen uses the most basic way of drawing up her profit-and-loss account.

Helen's profit-and-loss account for one month

	£		£
Overheads	800	Gross profit	1,360
Balance, i.e. net profit	560		
	1,360		1,360

Here we have assumed that Helen's enterprise is a limited company. Her salary of £350 is one of the overheads. If she were a sole trader, her remuneration of £350 a month would not be included in the £800 overheads, which would then fall to £450 a month. The month's net profit before tax would be £910 (£560 + £350).

You can make your account more informative by providing more detail: you can isolate and highlight items of overheads or other factors that you particularly want to keep an eye on: for example, the cost of power consumption. If power is a cost that varies with the volume of production, you could treat it as a materials purchase rather than an overhead.

Cash-flow forecast

However healthy a profit-and-loss account, it doesn't show whether you will be able to pay all the bills or when you will receive all the money due. Your suppliers may demand cash on delivery while your customers place orders on 30- or 60-day credit terms. You could have a cash-flow problem, especially if your business is expanding and demanding additional expenditure.

Drawing up a cash-flow forecast is explained in Chapter 3. The cash-flow examples in this chapter are simplified to illustrate the forecasting principles. They ignore VAT and assume equal monthly overheads. Here is Helen's latest cash-flow forecast.

Helen's latest cash-flow forecast [figures in square brackets show a deficit]

Month	Jan	Feb	Mar	Apr	May
	£	£	£	£	£
Opening bank balance/[overdraft]	[3,000]	[2,200]	[1,400]	[600]	200
Payments:					
purchases	2,000	2,000	2,000	2,000	2,000
labour	400	400	400	400	400
overheads	800	800	800	800	800
Maximum borrowing requirement	6,200	5,400	4,600	3,800	3,000
Receipts from sales	4,000	4,000	4,000	4,000	4,000
Closing balance/[overdraft]	[2,200]	[1,400]	[600]	200	1,000

Helen has now been asked to take on a regular order for another 200 units a month, but with payment only after 90 days. Helen will need to buy another machine for £500, pay additional part-time labour costs and needs two months to build up the manufacturing capacity. Helen prepares a forecast to decide whether to accept the order.

Helen's longer-term cash-flow forecast [figures in square brackets show a deficit]

Month	Jun	Jul	Aug	Sep	Oct	Nov	Dec
Products made	200	300	400	400	400	400	400
	£	£	£	£	£	£	£
Opening balance/ [overdraft]	1,000	300	[1,300]	[2,900]	[4,500]	[4,100]	[1,700]
Payments:							
purchases	3,000	4,000	4,000	4,000	4,000	4,000	4,000
labour	400	800	800	800	800	800	800
overheads	800	800	800	800	800	800	800
Capital expenditure	500						
Maximum borrowing requirement	3,700	5,300	6,900	8,500	10,100	9,700	7,300
Receipts from sales	4,000	4,000	4,000	4,000	6,000	8,000	8,000
Closing balance/ [overdraft]	300	[1,300]	[2,900]	[4,500]	[4,100]	[1,700]	700

This forecast shows that Helen would be overdrawn at the end of the five months from July to November. The overdraft would rise to £4,500 at the end of September and fall the following months when she starts to get payments from the new customer. The bank might be willing to lend this £4,500 in the light of Helen's track record. She managed to pay off a £3,000 overdraft in January by the end of April. To minimise her borrowing requirement, Helen might be able to persuade her suppliers to agree to a delayed payment. She might also be able to arrange payments in months when no major overheads are due.

The cost of additional power consumption resulting from increased production and the interest payable on a loan or overdrafts have been excluded from this simplified example. But even a simplified example gives an early approximation of what might be needed.

Helen's forecast shows that a large order and delayed payment by the customer could be a disaster if her business could not cover the expenditure needed for the additional output. Revise a cash-flow forecast whenever you expect a change in circumstances, particularly if you are thinking of expanding production.

Break-even point

Having forecast production in the next six months or so, work out the break-even point where receipts balance the costs. The business loses money before the break-even point, and is in profit after it. The break-even point is measured in units of production in a manufacturing business, in the number of paid hours worked in a service business.

The costs of manufacturing anything can be divided into two categories: fixed and variable. Fixed costs remain the same whatever the amount you manufacture: they comprise the overheads and, in the short term, labour. Variable costs vary with the amount you manufacture and include items such as materials and power.

Some costs are partly fixed and partly variable: for example, power. You are bound to use some power even without manufacturing anything and need extra the more you produce. Power costs should be split into their fixed and variable elements. In the following example, power is treated only as an overhead for the sake of simplicity.

The relationship between Ahmed's volume of production and profitability is shown below.

Ahmed's profit at each volume of production

Units made	Variable cost	Fixed cost	Total cost	Receipts from sales	Profit/ [loss]
40	400	2,400	2,800	800	[2,000]
120	1,200	2,400	3,600	2,400	[1,200]
200	2,000	2,400	4,400	4,000	[400]
280	2,800	2,400	5,200	5,600	400

These figures can be expressed in a graph. The horizontal axis represents the number of units produced; the vertical axis represents money. Ahmed plots the selling price and total cost at each volume of production. The two lines cross where production is 240 units. This is the break-even point. Beyond it, Ahmed is in profit.

A calculation and simple graph will enable you to plan your volume of production to take account of your financial resources. You can use graphs to show how fixed costs, variable costs, sales price and profits affect each other. You may, for example, wish to expand production to an extent that will increase your fixed costs. Can you maintain profits?

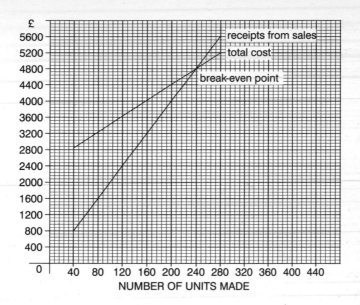

Balance sheet

A balance sheet lets you analyse your deployment of your resources and will be required by any substantial lender. You will need a year-end balance sheet and intermediate ones, or the details ready to compile balance sheets at regular intervals. You can observe the trend in any particular matter you want to analyse.

A balance sheet shows the financial state of the business at a given date. It takes account of what the business owns (its assets), and of what it owes (its liabilities). Both can be subdivided into fixed and current balances.

- *Fixed liabilities* are debts that are repayable over a long period of time.
- *Current liabilities* are those that must be repaid in the short term: for example, debts to suppliers, overdrafts and interest on loans.
- *Fixed assets* are property, such as land, buildings, plant, machinery and vehicles. These need to be revalued periodically, and their book-value adjusted. Land and buildings tend to increase in value with inflation (though not always). Plant, machinery and vehicles depreciate and have to be replaced. It is useful to set up a sinking fund or reserve for an eventual replacement cost.

- *Current assets* include customers' debts, the value of any stock held, and money in hand or in the bank.
- *Quick assets* are narrow current assets represented by money; by assets that can be quickly converted to money, such as Stock Exchange securities; and by some short-term debts of reliable customers. Raw materials are not included nor, generally, are finished goods.

Use up-to-date and realistic sale values for the assets. You can then convert the actual figures into a ratio or percentage of solvency. Balance sheet analysis can answer important questions about the business.

- Can it meet its commitments? Is it solvent?
- Can it pay its outside creditors in full, if necessary by selling all its assets and closing down?
- Can it pay current liabilities out of current assets as a going concern? What is the current ratio?
- Can it pay current liabilities out of quick assets? What is the quick ratio?

This current ratio would ideally be rather better than 1:1. You would have more current assets than current liabilities to give a prudent margin of safety. But current assets may not all be easily saleable. Excluding some current assets, the quick ratio will be less than the current ratio and often less than 1:1. Your accountant can advise on choosing ratios appropriate for your own business and about other useful analyses from the balance sheet.

Ahmed has financed his business with:

- £6,000 capital to start the business
- £5,000 profits kept in reserve to be used to buy additional plant and to provide additional working capital – he could invest his reserves if they are not needed immediately and enter them as investments on the asset side of the balance sheet
- £2,400 overdraft of a £4,000 overdraft facility
- £5,000 medium-term bank loan to buy plant and machinery.

Ahmed's balance sheet at 1 January 2003

	£	£	£
ASSETS			
Fixed assets:			
plant and machinery	13,000		
motor vehicles	8,000		
	21,000		
Less hire-purchase debt	4,000	17,000	
Current assets			
stock	2,000		
debtors	5,000	7,000	24,000
LIABILITIES:			
Medium-term bank loan		5,000	
Current liabilities:			
creditors	5,600		
overdraft	2,400	8,000	13,000
TOTAL NET ASSETS			11,000
Resources to generate these net assets:			
Ahmed's capital introduced into business		6,000	
Ahmed's undrawn profits left in business		5,000	
			11,000

Ahmed's balance sheet shows that the business was solvent on 1 January 2003 if he'd had to close down. It had assets of £24,000 and liabilities of £13,000, leaving total net assets of £11,000.

But Ahmed could not have met current liabilities of £8,000 out of current assets of £7,000. The current ratio was 1:1.14 (£8,000 divided by £7,000). And the current liabilities figure of £8,000 compares with a quick assets figure of £5,000, a £3,000 shortfall and a quick ratio of 1:1.6. Ahmed's balance sheet is weak. He has £1,600 of his unused overdraft facility, but dependence on renewal of overdraft arrangements makes the business vulnerable. A series of balance sheets on different dates might give a different impression. One balance sheet a year cannot ever be informative enough.

The balance sheet of a company would have to be drawn up differently from that of a sole trader or partnership. Its capital would be shown among the liabilities: it belongs to the shareholders, not the company. Likewise the net profit on the trading account must ultimately be distributed to shareholders. In a sole-trader firm or partnership, the capital investment and the profits are owned by the firm and count as assets.

Chapter 8

Sorting out tax

When you set up in business for yourself, you may have to pay some or all of income tax, corporation tax, Value Added Tax (VAT) and National Insurance. VAT is administered by Customs & Excise, the other taxes by the Inland Revenue. Tax rules and rates can change in the annual spring Budget and at other times, and your local tax enquiry centre (in the phone book under 'Inland Revenue') can be consulted for the latest figures. The Customs & Excise National Advice Line★ deals with queries on VAT.

You do not need to inform these departments separately about your affairs. Instead, ask for a copy of the leaflet *Starting Your Own Business?* (CWL1), which is available from the Inland Revenue or Customs & Excise. This contains an introduction to the taxes you might have to pay and lists other useful leaflets, helplines and further sources of advice. Complete form CWF1, which comes with the leaflet, and return it the Inland Revenue National Insurance Contributions Office at the address shown on the form; it will pass on your details to the relevant authorities. You may then be sent further forms to complete: for example, if you need or want to register for VAT.

Sole traders and partnerships

Sole traders and partners count as self-employed and pay income tax under Schedule D on business profits. You set your personal allowances against your total income, including business profits: on income above your allowances you pay tax at 10, 22 or 40 per cent. Once your income is above the relevant thresholds, you must also pay Class 2 and Class 4 National Insurance contributions.

The profits of a partnership are calculated in the same way as for a sole trader. The taxable profits are then split up between the partners, in line with the profit-sharing agreement in force for that year. So if, for example, the profits are £40,000 and there are two partners sharing them equally, each will get £20,000. Their individual tax bills will depend on their other income, reliefs and allowances. In effect, partners are treated as if they run their own individual business based on their share of the partnership profits. Partners are responsible for tax only on their own part of the profits.

Sources of assistance

You do not have to use an accountant or other tax adviser. However, a professional can guide you on the expenses and allowances you can claim to reduce your tax bill. You could consider paying for help for at least the first year or two, until you feel confident enough to do it yourself. (See Chapter 3 for how to find an accountant or tax adviser.) Accountants are fallible, and you are still responsible for declaring your income correctly. Keep an eye on what is being done in your name and try to understand it so that you can query your accountant.

The Inland Revenue has helplines and tax enquiry centres, which can help if you decide to sort out your tax affairs yourself. You could also use software such as *TaxCalc*, which helps you complete your tax return and work out your tax bill. Which? Books publishes *Which? Way To Save Tax* to take into account changes in the Chancellor's annual Budget.

Tax is made easier if your own book-keeping system is consistent with the Inland Revenue tax return. Ask your accountant, or ask for leaflet SA3 *Self-assessment: A Guide to Keeping Records for the Self-employed* from any tax office. It sets out the minimum length of time you have a legal duty to keep your accounts and all relevant documents. Your tax inspector has the right to ask for complete records of the whole of the firm's payments and receipts including what has been drawn for private expenditure, supported by invoices, receipts, bank records and statements, paying-in books and cheque stubs.

Accounting period

A firm's accounts are made up annually, though the first trading period may be shorter or longer than a year. It is usual to nominate the day you first close your books as your annual accounting date and to use this day as the end of the trading year for as long as the firm continues in business. You can decide which day is to be your year's end. It could coincide with the end of the tax (fiscal) year on 5 April, or with the end of the calendar year, or any other date that suits. Choosing your accounting date is an important decision. You can save tax by selecting the right date, but you will also want it to fit in with a timetable for calculating and declaring business profits which is convenient for you.

Tax for sole traders and partners is generally based on profits for the accounting year ending during the tax year. Tax years run from 6 April in one year to 5 April in the next year. Your first accounting period can be longer than 12 months. It could also be shorter if, for example, you start part-way through the tax year and want your accounting year to end at the same time as the end of the tax year. Special rules apply to the first – and sometimes the second – tax year of trading.

- *First tax year,* i.e. the tax year in which you start trading. You pay tax on the proportion of the profits in your first accounting period that falls into the first tax year of trading up to 5 April: for example, if you start in October and end your first accounting period 12 months later, you would pay tax on 6/12 of the profits in your first accounting year.
- *Second tax year.* You pay tax on the profits for the accounting period that ends in the second tax year. Sometimes there is no accounting period ending in the second tax year. This would be the case if your first accounting period lasted for longer than 12 months and happened to straddle three tax years. You could, for example, start in February 2003 and close your first accounting period in May 2004 after 15 months – straddling the tax years 2002–2003, 2003–2004 and 2004–2005. In this case, 12 months of your first accounting period would fall into the second tax year, 2003–2004. You would pay tax on the 12/15 of the profits in your first accounting period.
- *Third and subsequent years.* You pay tax on profits for the accounting year that ends in that tax year (i.e. on your profits for your last accounting period).

Here's an example. Fatima started in business on 6 September 2003, fixing 5 September 2004 as the end of her first accounting period. In her first accounting year, her taxable profits were £27,430; in the second year, £28,400; in the third year, £32,000.

Taxable profits on Fatima's first three accounting periods

tax year	accounting year period		taxable profits
	from	to	
2003–4	6–9–03	5–4–04	£16,000 ($7/_{12}$ of £27,430)
2004–5	6–9–03	5–9–04	£27,430
2005–6	6–9–04	5–9–05	£28,400
2006–7	6–9–05	5–9–06	£32,000

Some of the profits in Fatima's first accounting year have been taxed twice – £16,000. These are called overlap profits. Fatima will get overlap relief against this excessive taxation only when she ceases trading or changes her accounting date. It is better to carry forward as little overlap profit as possible, since inflation erodes the value of the relief. Generally speaking, therefore, you should either keep the first 12 months' profit as low as possible or choose your year-end carefully.

Choosing your accounting date

If you select fiscal accounting, you have no overlap profit and avoid the complications of opening-year rules. This means having an accounting year that coincides with the tax year: an end-March accounting date also qualifies. The drawbacks are that you have less time to draw up your accounts than if you choose an accounting date later in the year, and you will pay tax on the profits earlier.

Fatima, for example, makes her first tax payment on 31 January 2005, nearly five months after the end of her first accounting year on 5 September 2004. If her accounting date were 30 April 2004, the payment would not be due until nine months after her year-end. In any case, Fatima should budget for the fact that her January 2004 payment will include not only her tax so far but also her first payment on account for the 2004–5 tax year.

Another factor when selecting an accounting date is convenience. If you are registered for VAT, it keeps things simple if your accounting date coincides with the end of a VAT quarter. If your business is seasonal, consider ending your accounting year in a slack period.

Capital allowances

Capital expenditure is money spent on plant, buildings, machinery, vehicles and anything else that has an enduring benefit for the business and does not need to be renewed every year. You may qualify for capital allowances. They are calculated by putting the cost of the plant or machinery you buy into a pool of expenditure.

- Each year, you can claim up to 25 per cent of the value of the pool as a writing-down allowance, which can be deducted from your profits for that year.
- The pool is reduced by what you claim: what's left is the written-down value and becomes your pool for the start of the next accounting year. Any purchases for the next year are added to the pool, and at the end of the year you can claim 25 per cent of what the pool is then worth.
- You can claim less than the full writing-down allowance: this is worth doing if your profits are less than the potential allowance.
- On some items of capital expenditure, small- and medium-size businesses can claim 40 or 100 per cent of the cost as a capital allowance for the accounting year in which you incur the expenditure.
- If you sell something on which you have claimed capital allowance, the proceeds must be deducted from your pool of expenditure before working out your writing-down allowance for the year in which you sell.
- If the proceeds of all the items you sell come to more than the value of the pool, the excess (which is called a 'balancing charge') is added to your profits for the year and taxed.
- Most expenditure goes into one common pool. However, any car costing more than £12,000 must be kept in its own separate pool, with a maximum writing-down allowance of £3,000 a year.
- Items used partly for business, partly for private use, should be pooled separately because you can claim only the proportion of the expenditure that is in line with business use.
- You can elect for many capital items with an expected life of less than five years – computers, say – to be treated as short-life

assets. Each one is put into its own pool of expenditure. As long as use of them stops within the five years, you get immediate tax relief for any disposal (instead of having to wait until the business ceases, as you do with assets in your main pool).

Capital allowances can be complicated. It would be worth consulting an accountant or tax adviser if you are thinking of a substantial capital purchase.

Business expenses

Any expenses that are not capital expenditure and that are incurred wholly and exclusively for the purposes of carrying on the business can be set off against tax. There is no definitive list of 'allowable' expenses, but items of expenditure that are generally permitted include:

- pay and employer's pension contributions of staff employed in the business, including pay to members of your family if they are genuinely employed and it is a fair rate for the type and amount of work they do
- expenses of business travel, but not the cost of going to and from home to the main place of work
- interest on loans taken out for the acquisition or running of a business
- interest charges on hire-purchase of capital equipment
- hire or leasing of equipment
- spending on research and development, which is classed as 'scientific research'
- insurance premiums
- bad debts
- subscriptions to trade and professional associations
- general overheads, such as telephone, heating and lighting, advertising, stationery and postage
- accountancy fees, bank charges, etc.

You may claim a proportion of the expenses such as rent, phone, light, heating for things that are used partly for business and partly for private use if, for example, you use your home for business. You can claim the appropriate portion of the costs of running of a car, including a capital allowance. Keep a record of the business mileage and the total mileage. If your turnover is below the VAT-registration threshold, you can work out the costs on a 'cost per business mile' basis, provided the rate per mile does not exceed that in the 'Fixed Profit Car Scheme' scales published periodically by the Inland Revenue. But if you choose this option, you cannot claim capital allowances as well, and you must stick with this method until you change your car.

Losses

Many businesses make losses in their early years. An accountant can advise on the best way to use them to reduce overall tax. The various options can produce different results and can also affect your cash flow.

Sole traders and partners who make a loss in the first four years of trading can set it against other income received in the three tax years before the trading loss was incurred. Tax paid in the earlier tax year will be refunded.

However long you have been in business, you can set a loss against any other income received in the same tax year or in the preceding tax year. If losses exceed income, the excess can be set against any capital gains for the given year. You can also carry a loss forward to set against future business profits.

Tax returns and paying tax

You have to declare your income, expenses and profits on your tax return each year. Tax returns are sent out each April. There are important deadlines that you must meet or risk paying penalties: for example, you must send in your tax return by 31 January after the end of the tax year. You may be sent a return without having to ask for one. If you don't receive one, you have until 5 October after the end of the tax year to tell your tax office that you have income on which tax is due. You will then be sent a tax return.

You need to put various business figures on the tax return, though if your turnover is below £15,000 a year you should enter just your turnover, allowable expenses and the resulting profit. You can work out your own tax bill or ask the Inland Revenue to calculate the tax you owe whenever you send back your tax return.

Aim to return it by 30 September. Your tax office won't guarantee to work out your bill in time for the 31 January payment deadline if you miss the 30 September cut-off. You could then end up paying tax late and you'll be charged interest.

Tax is due in instalments. The first payment for the tax year is due on 31 January, nearly ten months into the tax year. The second payment for the tax year is due on 31 July, nearly four months after the end of the tax year. These two payments are 'on account' and based on your tax bill for the previous year (or an estimate, if your first accounting period has not yet ended). A third (balancing) payment will be due on 31 January nearly ten months after the end of the tax year, once your actual tax bill for the tax year has been worked out. You'll get a credit against the payment on account for the following year if the payments on account come to more than the actual bill.

Capital profits

You can make capital profits by, for example, selling business property or goodwill, and this may make you liable to capital gains tax (CGT). Calculating a tax liability on the disposal of a business asset and the reliefs available can be complex, so consider getting help from an accountant.

The main reliefs available against capital gains are as follows.

- *Indexation allowance* deducts any gains due to inflation since March 1982. There is no indexation allowance after April 1998. Instead you get *taper relief*, which reduces the rate of tax payable in line with the length of time you have held the asset.
- *Capital losses* can be set against gains.
- *Tax-free allowance.* There is no tax on otherwise taxable gains up to the annual capital gains tax exemption each year.
- *Roll-over relief* allows you to defer a capital gains tax bill when you dispose of 'qualifying' business assets and reinvest an amount equal to the disposal proceeds in a new qualifying asset within three years after, or one year before, the disposal. Qualifying assets include land or property, goodwill and fixed plant or machinery.

- *Reinvestment in enterprise investment scheme shares* defers capital gains tax.
- *Hold-over relief* defers capital gains tax if you give away business assets or shares in an unquoted company: for example, by passing them on to younger members of your family.

Self-employed National Insurance

If you are a sole trader or a partner, you pay Class 2 National Insurance contributions at a flat rate of £2 a week by quarterly bills or monthly direct debit. You can claim exemption from Class 2 payments if you are able to show that your net earnings from self-employment in a tax year are expected to be below a certain sum (£4,095 in the 2003–4 tax year). You must apply to the Inland Revenue for a certificate of exemption in advance.

In addition, you have to pay Class 4 National Insurance contributions if your taxable profits exceed a certain sum (£4,615 in the 2003–4 tax year). The rate is 8 per cent up to a certain limit (£30,940 in 2003–4) and 1 per cent above the limit. The amount you pay is worked out after you have filled in your tax return and is added to your income tax bill.

Should you start your business in your spare time while continuing to work for an employer, you must pay all three types of contribution – Class 1, Class 2 and Class 4. Anything you pay over an upper limit in a tax year will be refunded.

Companies

If your business is a limited company, you as one of its directors are still an employee. At the start of each trading year, you determine what your annual salary will be and pay it to yourself monthly or weekly. You can wait until you know the full year's trading before fixing directors' overall remuneration – salary, perks, dividends and employer's (that is, the company's) contribution to the pension. Choose the best mix to achieve a balance between minimising the company's corporation tax and setting the directors' personal tax as low as possible, bearing in mind their personal tax allowances and any other income. A director's remuneration can also include benefits in kind such as company cars and dividends on his or her shares in the company.

Each pay-day you deduct income tax and Class 1 National Insurance contributions from all employees' pay, including your own, under the PAYE (Pay-As-You-Earn) system. You must also pay employer's National Insurance contributions. These payroll deductions are usually sent to the Inland Revenue every month. Sometimes they may be paid on a quarterly basis.

Corporation tax

Corporation tax is paid on profits – what's left after salaries, bonuses and all other expenses have been paid. At the end of the trading year, you can decide what to do with any profit. This could be retained in the business, taken as additional salary or bonus or paid as a dividend to the shareholders. Dividends are liable to corporation tax, but not National Insurance. There may be an advantage in paying a dividend before the end of the trading year: your accountant should be able to advise you on this.

In the 2002–3 tax year, corporation tax rates were as follows.

- Companies with profits below £10,000 pay no corporation tax.
- Companies with profits between £10,000 and £50,000 pay corporation tax on a rate that increases according to the level of profits until it reaches 19 per cent, which is the small-companies rate paid by those whose profits are between £50,000 and £300,000.
- Above £300,000, corporation tax increases gradually to 30 per cent. This is the main corporation tax rate for companies with profits of £1.5 million or more.

These rates may have changed in the 2003 spring Budget after we went to press.

Accounting period

A company may choose any date for its accounting period, which cannot be more than 12 months long. Corporation tax is charged by reference to the fiscal financial year, which runs from 1 April to 31 March. A company's accounting period is often different, so profits have to be apportioned between two tax years. A company that uses January to December as its accounting period, for example, would have 3/12 of its profits in one year and 9/12 in the other. Tax due is calculated on the basis of the accounting period within which the profits fall, rather than tax years.

Capital allowances, expenses and losses

Business expenses and capital allowances are the same for companies as for sole traders and partnerships (see above), though first-year capital allowances may be less generous for large companies. Capital allowances must be set against the company's income.

A company's trading loss can be set against its profits in the previous year or carried forward indefinitely to set against profits from the same trade in subsequent years.

Tax returns and paying tax

Companies must complete an annual company tax return and are also required to keep comprehensive records. Corporation tax is due nine months from the end of the accounting period, for example in September in the case of a January to December accounting period.

Capital profits

Limited companies do not pay capital gains tax on capital profit. They pay corporation tax calculated broadly in line with the capital gains tax rules (see above). Unlike sole traders and partners, companies continue to get indexation allowance after April 1998, but they cannot claim reinvestment relief through the Enterprise Investment Scheme (see Chapter 2).

Value added tax

Value Added Tax (VAT) tax is levied on the supply of most goods and services in the UK and is normally payable quarterly to Customs & Excise. The tax you pay on goods and services that you buy for your business is called input tax, while the tax you charge your customers is called output tax.

This is how VAT works: you buy raw materials for £235 (made up of £200 plus £35 VAT at 17.5 per cent): £35 is your input tax. You use the materials to manufacture products you sell for £528.75 (made up of £450 plus £78.75 VAT at 17.5 per cent): £78.75 is your output tax. You deduct the input tax from the output tax and pay the balance of £43.75 to Customs & Excise. If your input tax is greater than your output tax, you claim a refund from Customs & Excise.

There are four categories of goods and services. These are:

- *exempt* – VAT is not payable under any circumstances (e.g., insurance, doctors' services)
- *zero-rated* – in theory, the goods and services are subject to VAT but no VAT is charged because the tax rate is 0 per cent (e.g., some exported goods and food in shops)
- *reduced-rated* – VAT at 5 per cent (e.g. domestic fuel and some energy-saving installations)
- *standard-rated* – VAT at 17.5 per cent (on most goods and services).

The difference between exempt and zero-rated may seem theoretical but has practical consequences. You cannot claim refunds of input tax unless you are registered for VAT and collecting output tax, if only notionally at the zero rate. If you sell only exempt supplies, you would not be a *taxable person* and could not register for VAT. You could not then claim back the input tax you pay on any supplies you buy, such as the VAT on your phone bills and stationery.

Compulsory registration for VAT

You must register for VAT if, at the end of any month, you have sold taxable supplies above the registration threshold in the past 12 months or if you expect your taxable supplies to exceed the threshold in the next 30 days alone. The registration threshold is £55,000 as we go to press (but is likely to change). Zero-rated supplies count towards the total but exempt supplies do not. Contact your local Customs & Excise VAT office to get the registration forms.

You must include VAT in the prices you charge customers as soon as you register, but do not show VAT as a separate item in your invoices until you have received a VAT registration number. Within 30 days of getting your registration number, send out replacement invoices with VAT shown separately to VAT-registered customers, who will want to claim back the VAT.

You must keep accurate records of all transactions, including invoices you send and receive, which show payment of VAT. Keep them available for inspection by Customs & Excise at any time. You also have to make quarterly returns showing your input and output tax. There are penalties for defaulting on payments, or for failing to register for VAT on time. VAT leaflet 700/1 *Should I Be Registered for VAT?* explains in detail the compulsory registration rules.

Buying a VAT-registered business

You must also register if you buy a going concern from a VAT-registered trader. You may be allowed to use the same VAT registration number, but consider this only after discussion with your accountant or solicitor as it would make you liable for VAT owed by the previous business. It is important to get the registration sorted out before you sign the contract to buy the business. The leaflet *Transfer of a Business as a Going Concern* (700/9) may help; it is available from your VAT office.

You can apply to deregister if you intend to run the business on a smaller scale and decide that VAT registration has no advantage.

Voluntary registration for VAT

You can register for VAT even if your taxable supplies are below the registration limit. Voluntary registration can have advantages.

- You can claim back all your input tax, for example on equipment you buy when setting up. This reduces your business costs.
- You should be able to maintain more stable prices if you register for VAT right from the start – even though your turnover does not yet require it – than if you do so only once your turnover has grown to the point where you must register, because VAT will increase all your prices. This could unsettle your customers if they cannot claim back VAT. Voluntary registration is also more attractive if your customers are VAT-registered businesses, since they can simply claim back whatever VAT you charge.
- You will improve your cash flow in the short term. You'll have more cash flowing into the business, though it will eventually have to be paid to Customs & Excise. You can claim back VAT

on supplies you buy when you receive the invoice. This could be some time before you have to pay for the goods if your supplier gives you extended credit. But this advantage becomes a disadvantage if you give credit to customers. You may have to pay your output tax to Customs & Excise before the customer pays you.

Voluntary registration for VAT also has other potential disadvantages.

- VAT puts up your costs to general consumers and may put you at a competitive disadvantage
- VAT adds to your workload, or costs if you use an accountant, because of the record-keeping and accounting generated by VAT.

If you register and find that the disadvantages outweigh the advantages, you can cancel your registration if the taxable supplies you sell are below the current deregistration limit, normally a couple of thousand pounds or so below the compulsory registration limit. VAT leaflet *Deregistering for VAT* (700/1) explains the rules.

Pre-registration expenses

You can claim back up to six months' input tax on purchases made before you registered for VAT, providing various conditions are met. If you start a business in which you intend to produce taxable supplies in the future, you can apply for VAT registration beforehand. You will need evidence of firm arrangements to make taxable supplies such as contracts, licences and planning permission. You will be able to claim back input tax that is wholly attributable to the intended taxable supplies.

Cash-accounting scheme

Cash accounting is open to all firms whose taxable supplies (excluding VAT) do not exceed £350,000. Under this scheme you pay VAT on the basis of money actually paid and received rather than on the date of invoices. It helps businesses that give extended credit to customers, as they not need to hand over VAT on credit transactions until they have received payment, and they automatically get relief for bad debt. Businesses not in the scheme have to apply for VAT relief on bad debt.

Retail schemes

Retail schemes for VAT are intended for shopkeepers and other retail traders, for whom the system of issuing a tax invoice for each sale would be impracticable. There is a choice of retail schemes. Consult your VAT office and accountant before deciding which is best.

Annual accounting scheme

This is open to traders who have already been registered for at least one year, and whose annual taxable turnover (excluding VAT) does not exceed £300,000. It works like this: your VAT liability is estimated on the basis of the previous year's payments, and divided into ten monthly portions. Nine of these you pay by direct debit. You then have two months to send in your annual VAT return, and make the tenth (balancing) payment.

This system means that you have to make only one return a year, instead of four. Knowing in advance how much you are going to be paying, you are spared unpleasant jolts to your cash-flow calculations. The balancing payment is less predictable, but you have an extra month's grace.

Businesses with a very low turnover (£100,000 a year or less) have a further option. You need make no interim payments if your previous year's net VAT liability was under £2,000. If it was over £2,000, you can make three quarterly payments of 20 per cent of the previous year's net VAT liability, and then a balancing payment.

Flat-rate scheme

You can usually opt for the flat-rate scheme if your taxable supplies are £150,000 (from April 2003) or less. You charge your customers the standard VAT rate of 17.5 per cent output tax but pass on a lower percentage to Customs & Excise – the amount being fixed according to the type of business you are in. The advantage is that you don't need VAT records for all the input tax on your purchases and expenses as you can't claim it back. Instead, you retain the difference between the 17.5 per cent you receive from your customers and the flat rate you pay to Customs & Excise. Even under the flat-rate scheme, you can claim back input tax on capital expenditure of £2,000 or more including VAT, if it's all on one invoice. If you subsequently sell the item, you must hand over the full 17.5 per cent output tax you add to the sale price.

The flat-rate scheme reduces record-keeping and the costs involved in adding up all your input and output tax when you fill out your VAT return – though you'll still need to keep similar records for income or corporation tax. Under the flat-rate scheme, you could be financially better off if you have relatively little input tax to claim back. However, if you have a lot of input tax to claim, you could end up with less cash in the bank. The attraction of the scheme all depends on the level at which the flat rate is set for your particular type of business, so you should discuss its relative advantages with your accountant.

The VAT leaflet *Flat-rate Scheme for Small Businesses* (733) gives details, flat rates for different types of business and an application form for the scheme.

Chapter 9

Employing others

Many one-person businesses – such as plumbers, hairdressers, photographers, consultants – remain just that. Other businesses start on a small-scale but eventually expand and so need to take on employees, while a few new business are designed from the planning stage to involve employees. As an employer, you have a range of extra responsibilities and laws to comply with.

Recruiting staff

When you have decided to take on employees, start by defining exactly what their duties are to be and what experience, skills and qualities are required to do the job. Be realistic about the sort of person who is likely to take the job, and avoid the temptation to ask for more skills and qualifications than are necessary – doing so may put off suitable but less-qualified people from applying and result in over-qualified applicants refusing the offer of a job. Get proof of qualifications and take up any references you ask for, preferably in writing. A good working relationship is much more likely to develop if both you and your workers are suited to each other. Ways of finding suitable employees include:

- government-run Jobcentres – for free help with recruitment
- private employment agencies – which charge the employer a fee
- advertisements in the local, national or trade press or on local radio stations
- postcard advertisements in local shops
- a notice outside your place of business
- personal recommendation.

Wherever they are placed, job particulars and advertisements must not exclude anyone on grounds of race, sex, marital status or disability, except in a very few closely defined cases. The more details you give in an advertisement, the less the chance that you will waste time dealing with applicants who won't want the job even if you want them. You should include:

- a description of your business including its size and what it does
- exact duties of the job
- promotion prospects
- experience, skills, qualifications and qualities you want in applicants
- training available
- place of work
- working hours
- pay
- holiday entitlement
- extra benefits, if any
- how to apply, with a closing date for applications.

It is sometimes easier and more economical to contract casual, part-time or freelance workers than to employ full-time permanent staff. Flexible hours are attractive to some people: for example, those with family commitments who are keen to get jobs that can be done partly at home or who don't want to work during school holidays.

Professional help with recruitment

Jobcentres can provide a free recruitment service for a wide range of jobs across all business sectors, can advise on staff selection and supply information on employment legislation. Ask whether you could benefit from any of the government's special schemes for promoting employment: for example, the New Deal scheme (www.newdeal.gov.uk) offers initial subsidies for employers who take on long-term unemployed people.

If you are seeking a worker with a particular skill that is in short supply locally, Jobcentres can circulate the vacancy widely, to attract people from other areas. Both Jobcentres and various private employment agencies list vacancies on their websites. A good site to start with is that of the Federation of Recruitment and Employment Services,★ the trade association for employment agencies.

You may, however, decide to employ young people and train them yourself. For workers aged under 18, you need to make a formal assessment of the risks arising from the work, giving a copy to the parent if the child is under 16. Consult your local careers service office about this and for advice on training. General information about training your staff (including small-firm training awards and loans) is available from Business Link★ (or the alternatives outside England).

Avoiding ineligible workers

Check that your employees are not working illegally – you risk prosecution if you take on someone who is not entitled to work in the UK. Acceptable checks include seeing a P45, P60 or payslip showing a National Insurance number (but not a temporary number, indicated by the letters TN). The Home Office Employers' Helpline★ can give further information.

Workers with particular skills may already be employed elsewhere and you may try to lure them away with terms that are in some way an improvement on what they are receiving or can get in their present jobs. Make sure their existing contracts of employment do not prohibit them from leaving to take up a similar job within a certain distance of the existing workplace. Otherwise, you both could end up with a costly court case.

Employee rights

It is important for new employers to familiarise themselves with employees' legal rights. These apply to both full- and part-time employees. You should also aim to keep abreast of regular changes in employment legislation, as some may add to the costs of running your business and will need to be budgeted for. A good source for more detailed information is the Advisory, Conciliation and Arbitration Service (ACAS).★ Their head office is in London, but offices in Scotland, Wales and in the English regions will deal with written and telephone enquiries. (Their addresses and telephone numbers can be found in local phone books.)

Although ACAS has a public profile as a conciliator in industrial disputes and those between individuals and their employers, it can also give advice to employers and employees on the complications of employment law. Another of its roles is to promote good industrial relations and prevent problems arising, and it can arrange visits by its advisers to employers' premises.

ACAS publishes booklets on recruitment and selection, workplace communications, job evaluation, discipline at work, and other aspects of employment. *Employing People* is written specially for small firms. It covers a range of employment matters including hiring staff, employment contracts, absence from work and unfair dismissal. All their booklets are available from ACAS Reader Ltd.★

Another source of information is the Department of Trade & Industry (DTI)'s★ Tiger service – a memorable but somewhat contrived acronym that stands for Tailored Interactive Guidance on Employment Rights. Tiger's website is at www.tiger.gov.uk. The DTI's leaflet *Individual Rights of Employees: a Guide for Employers and Employees* (01/1345) and a range of other useful publications are available from the DTI Publications Orderline★ and from Jobcentres.

The subject of employment law is among many courses run by Capita Learning & Development.★ Which? Books publishes *The Which? Guide to Employment*, which covers many of the issues in this chapter in more detail.

Statement of employment terms

You must give every worker who is taken on for at least a month a written statement setting out the conditions and terms on which he or she is employed. This is commonly called a contract of employment, though this is strictly not correct: the actual contract was formed earlier, when you made someone a definite offer of a job – orally or in writing – and it was firmly accepted.

Some things may form part of the contract even if they are not written down. All employment contracts, for example, are taken to require that you and your employee should act in good faith towards each other. Other unwritten conditions can become part of the contract by custom and practice, if they are reasonable and have generally applied in your area or trade for some time.

The written statement must be given within two months of starting work and contain information on at least the following:

- name of the employer and employee
- date of starting employment (and, possibly, the start date for employment with the previous employer if it counts as part of one continuous period of employment)
- title of job or description of employee's job
- rates of pay (including any overtime) and how they are calculated
- whether payment is to be provided by cheque, cash or bank transfer
- when payment is to be made (weekly or monthly)
- hours of work (regular and overtime, if applicable)
- holidays and holiday pay
- sick pay arrangements
- pension scheme arrangements
- length of notice required from employer and from employee
- rules relating to disciplinary procedures (if you have 20 or more employees)
- length of employment and end date – if not permanent
- place of work
- collective agreements
- rules relating to requirements to work outside the UK.

If any of these points do not apply – for example, if there are no pension arrangements – the written statement must say so explicitly. The terms set out in the statement can only rarely be altered without the consent of both parties. You may need to provide a new written statement if you promote an employee or transfer an employee to another kind of work. See *Written Statement of Employment Particulars* (00/1038) from the DTI Publications Orderline.★

Many employers confirm an oral offer of a job with a letter that sets out the conditions and terms. This letter counts as the written statement if it covers all the points above. If it doesn't, a written statement will still be necessary.

Paying your staff

Men and women doing the same or broadly similar work are entitled to the same rates of pay, and the national minimum wage is the least you must pay an employee. Those aged 18 to 21 should receive at least £3.60 an hour, while older workers get £4.10 an hour.

These rates apply from October 2002 and are likely to be revised each October. The national minimum wage is fairly straightforward to apply in many businesses, but in some there are complications: for example, in businesses where you supply accommodation to the employee you may be able to count part of the cost of providing accommodation as a proportion of the minimum wage. See *A Detailed Guide to the National Minimum Wage* (01/1144) from the DTI Publications Orderline.★

Apart from the national minimum wage, there may be an agreement between the employers' federation of your trade and the appropriate trade unions, which may be binding on you. Find out what similar businesses in the area pay and whether pay is related to a union rate.

An accountant can show you how to set up a wages book, and may take on the job of looking after your payroll. The DTI's★ Small Business Service provides an automated Payroll Service to new small-business employers.

On each pay day, you must give each employee a pay-slip showing gross pay, deductions (with the reason given for each, such as income tax, National Insurance contributions, union subs) and the net pay. Keep a copy for your own records. If you pay in cash, get your copy signed by the employee as a receipt. See *Pay Statements: What They Must Itemise* (02/771) from the DTI Publications Orderline.

Working hours and paid holiday

Working-time regulations govern the hours that employees spend at work and apply to agency and temporary staff. They do not cover workers in a few areas, notably transport and those who work at sea. For detailed information and a leaflet, contact the Workright Information Line.★

Here are the main regulations that you need to understand.

- You cannot require employees to work more than an average of 48 hours a week. These hours are averaged over 17 weeks (extended in some cases), so 12-hour shifts would be permitted so long as the overall limits are not breached.
- Employees are entitled to one day off a week (two if aged 16 or 17).
- Employees can voluntarily agree not to apply the weekly hours limit. If this happens, keep records of hours worked. If you

employ 20 or fewer workers and want to make an agreement with them as a whole, each employee must sign the agreement. There are also safeguards to prevent staff from discrimination or abuse if they want to keep to the limit.

- There are rules covering rest breaks, including a requirement for 11 hours of consecutive rest a day and a minimum 20-minute break if the working day is more than 6 hours. More rests are required for younger employees and there are special rules for night workers. Employees cannot agree to alter rest-break rules. In some cases, there is flexibility for the rest-break rules: for example, in security work and care work or where there is a foreseeable surge in activity in a business such as in tourism. You must provide adequate rest to compensate. And there is a *force majeure* provision to cope with unexpected and unpredictable occurrences beyond your control.
- Employees are entitled to a minimum of four weeks' paid annual holiday (or pro rata for part-time employees). You can include bank holidays in the minimum.

Employees whose working time is not measured or pre-determined, such as managing executives and family workers, are effectively covered only by the rules about annual paid leave.

You should allow time off to employees engaged on some trade union or public duties: for example, justices of the peace, local councillors, school governors. A pregnant employee has the right to time off for visits to antenatal clinics. Staff are allowed time off for job-hunting or training if you are making them redundant. Time off should be with pay, unless it is for public duties or some trade union activities. See *Time Off for Job Hunting or to Arrange Training When Facing Redundancy* (99/947) and *Time Off for Public Duties* (00/1402) from the DTI Publications Orderline.*

Pregnancy and parenting

You will have to pay an employee statutory maternity pay (SMP) for up to 26 weeks from the 11th week before the baby is due if she:

- has been working for you continuously for at least 26 weeks ending with the 15th week before the baby is due (this 15th week is known as the qualifying week)

- has average weekly earnings of not less than the lower earnings limit for the payment of National Insurance contributions
- is still pregnant in the 11th week before the baby is due, or must have already given birth (there are special regulations for premature births)
- has actually stopped work
- has given you proper advance notice of her intentions.

Employers who pay £20,000 a year or less in gross National Insurance contributions can deduct all SMP from the National Insurance they are due to pay. Other employers may reclaim only 92 per cent of SMP. See CA29 *SMP Manual for Employers* from the Inland Revenue for a detailed explanation of these rules and current rates of maternity pay.

Maternity leave

However short her service with you, a pregnant employee has a right to 18 weeks' maternity leave (longer in a few cases). During this leave she retains all her normal terms and conditions of employment except pay. A woman who has worked for you for at least two years by the beginning of the 11th week before her baby is due is entitled to additional maternity leave – up to the end of the 28th week after the week in which her child is born. However, her normal terms and conditions of employment do not automatically apply – it depends on her contract of employment.

An employee who has worked for you for at least a year by the 11th week before the baby was due is entitled to return to work (unless the business has five or fewer employees). She is entitled to her former job at the end of her leave or, if her post has become redundant, a suitable alternative job.

Parental leave

Employees who have worked for you for a year can take:

- 13 weeks' unpaid leave to care for a child in its first five years
- two weeks' leave on statutory paternity when a baby has been born or a child adopted (for fathers)
- 26 weeks' leave on statutory adoption pay when they adopt
- reasonable unpaid leave to sort out family problems and emergencies.

Flexible work

Parents can ask for flexible working arrangements in the first five years of a child's life, or the first 18 years if a child is disabled. Employers are obliged to consider such a request, which can be declined providing you can show good reasons for doing so if the employee takes the matter to a tribunal.

When employees fall ill

A contract of employment should show how much and in what circumstances you will pay sick pay. You cannot pay less than a legal minimum. Under the statutory sick pay (SSP) scheme, an employer must pay employees sick pay for up to 28 weeks' illness. Spells of illness shorter than four days (including Saturdays, Sundays and holidays) do not qualify for sick pay, nor do the first three days of sickness.

The 28-week maximum may be made up of intermittent linked periods of illness and cover more than one tax year, provided that the gap between any periods is not more than eight weeks. Whether the illness is in linked periods or a continuous period, your obligation ceases after 28 weeks and state benefit takes over. However, your obligation starts again if, having recovered, the employee should fall ill again more than eight weeks after the end of a maximum period.

If you have a high proportion of your workforce sick, you can reclaim some of the SSP under the percentage threshold scheme. Should you have paid out more than 13 per cent of the total of your employers' and employees' Class 1 National Insurance contributions for that month, you can claim back any SSP amount over and above 13 per cent.

You don't have to give sick pay to people who earn less than the National Insurance lower earnings limit nor to employees over 65. See CA30 *SSP Manual for Employers* from the Inland Revenue for a detailed explanation of these rules and current rates of sick pay.

The government Employers' Helpline* provides free advice to employers about statutory sick pay, statutory maternity pay and National Insurance contributions. This service is particularly aimed at new or established small businesses without a separate wages department.

Pensions

You can choose whether or not to set up a pension scheme for your employees. Many small employers do not bother because of the cost, administration and time involved. However, you are obliged at least to give your employees access to a stakeholder pension if you have five or more employees. This itself may not be too onerous. It involves making details of the scheme available to employees and deducting contributions from pay, sending these to the pension provider and keeping appropriate records. Pension companies such as insurance companies and financial advisers can give advice.

Suspending employees

If business is bad, you may want to put some employees on short time, or even lay them off without pay or with pay at a lower rate. Your right to do so should be specified at the time of engaging an employee. Most employees are entitled to a small guaranteed payment for up to five working days in any three months in which you have no work for them to do. See *Guarantee Payments* (00/902) from the DTI Publications Orderline.★

Making employees redundant

Staff may have to be made redundant when a firm is not doing sufficient business to justify their employment. A redundancy dismissal can be unfair on the basis of improper selection, lack of consultation and insufficient notice. Redundancy should not be motivated by personal reasons: for example, because you would prefer to lose women rather than men. Workers who think you are making them redundant just to get rid them can challenge your decision at an employment tribunal.

An employer who makes 20 or more people redundant must inform the Department of Trade and Industry (DTI).★ Get the appropriate form from your local Employment Service office or order the leaflet *Redundancy Consultation and Notification* (02/1141) from the DTI Publications Orderline.★

An employer must consult with the trade union at the earliest opportunity if the employees are members of a union. When 10 to 99 redundancies are proposed within a 30-day period, employers must enter into at least 30 days' consultation with the trade union before the first dismissal takes place.

Redundancy pay is due to those employees who have at least two years' continuous service. Service given before the age of 18 does not count. For more details see *Redundancy Payments* (PL808), available from the Redundancy Payments Service,* which also operates a free helpline.

Redundancy after you buy a business

One important point to be aware of if you take over a going concern is that workers' employment is deemed in law to be continuing. So if you plan to make existing staff redundant when you take over a business, you may find yourself landed with a large bill for redundancy pay. Before buying a business, get a list of all employees showing their length of continuous employment there, so you can assess the cost of possible redundancy pay and negotiate with the seller of the business about which of you is to pay. For further details see *Employment Rights on Transfer of an Undertaking* (02/982) from the DTI Publications Orderline.*

Notice to end employment

An employee who has worked for you for one month or more is entitled to a week's notice or a week's pay in lieu of notice, unless the contract of employment specified a longer period of notice. After two years, you must give one week's notice for each year the employee has worked for you, up to a maximum of 12 weeks. After two years, an employee is entitled to request a written statement detailing the reason for being dismissed.

Unfair dismissal

A dismissed employee may bring a complaint of unfair dismissal to an employment tribunal after a minimum of one year's continuous employment. However, there is no qualifying period for employees who allege that they were dismissed because of trade union activity or for non-membership of a union, because of sex, disability or race discrimination, pregnancy or childbirth, or because they asserted their entitlement to one of their legal employment rights.

The tribunal will take account of the firm's size and resources when deciding whether a dismissal was fair or not, and whether to direct re-employment. A worker who is not up to the physical demands of the job, for example, can be dismissed by a small firm that may not have another job to offer. See *Dismissal: Fair or Unfair?* (02/506) from the DTI Publications Orderline.*

The need for good discipline

Transparent rules benefit both employer and employees by setting standards of conduct at work and making clear to employees what is expected of them. Employees will more readily accept regulations if care is taken to explain why they are necessary. Rules should cover such matters as timekeeping, absence, health and safety, race and sex discrimination and use of company facilities such as phones, photocopiers and email.

The rules should also specify the kind of offences that will be regarded as gross misconduct and which could lead to dismissal without notice. These could include serious offences such as physical violence, theft or fraud and other things that might arise from the particular type of business you run.

Disciplinary procedures

Disciplinary procedures can help to ensure that disciplinary offences are dealt with fairly and consistently, as well as minimising disagreements about disciplinary matters and reducing the need for dismissals. This may be particularly important if an employee should complain to an employment tribunal of unfair dismissal, as the employer will need to show the tribunal that the dismissal was fair.

The ACAS advisory handbook *Discipline at Work* gives practical advice on handling disciplinary matters with examples of rules and disciplinary procedures. It also publishes a code of practice, *Disciplinary Practice and Procedures in Employment.* Contact ACAS Reader Ltd* for copies.

The ACAS code states that disciplinary procedures should:

- be in writing
- specify to whom they apply
- provide for matters to be dealt with quickly
- indicate the disciplinary actions that may be taken
- specify the levels of management that have the authority to take the various forms of disciplinary action, ensuring that

immediate superiors do not normally have the power to dismiss without reference to senior management

- provide for individuals to be informed of the complaints against them and to be given an opportunity to state their case before decisions are reached
- give individuals the right to be accompanied by a trade union representative, or by a fellow employee of their choice, when stating their case
- ensure that, except for gross misconduct, no employees are dismissed for a first breach of discipline
- ensure that disciplinary action is not taken until the case has been carefully investigated
- ensure that individuals are given an explanation for any penalty imposed
- provide a right of appeal and specify the procedure to be followed.

In addition, disciplinary procedures should:

- apply to all employees, irrespective of their length of service
- be non-discriminatory
- ensure that any investigatory period of suspension is with pay, and specify how pay is to be calculated during such a period (if, exceptionally, suspension is to be without pay, this should be provided for in the contract of employment)
- ensure that, where the facts are in dispute, no disciplinary penalty is imposed until the case has been carefully investigated and it has been concluded, on the balance of probability, that the employee committed the act in question.

Disciplinary penalties

Informal action, such as counselling, should generally precede formal warnings. If an informal approach fails, then formal penalties are normally implemented progressively. There are typically four stages:

- oral warning
- first written warning
- final written warning
- dismissal.

While there are normally three stages before actual dismissal, they may be dispensed with if the employee's alleged misconduct warrants such action.

Trade unions

Employees have the right both to belong and not to belong to a trade union, and you cannot penalise or dismiss them for this. A trade union official also has a right to time off for some duties. Employers with more than 20 employees must officially recognise a trade union and comply with the rules that recognition brings, if the majority of the workforce want recognition. See *Union Membership Rights of Members and Non-members* (01/1378) from the DTI Publications Orderline.★

Anti-discrimination laws

There are laws about sex, race and disability discrimination in employment, some of which apply both to employees and job applicants. Other laws protect workers from reprisal if they blow the whistle on employers who breach the law, endanger health and safety or damage the environment. You can get further information from the Equal Opportunities Commission★ (sex discrimination), the Commission for Racial Equality★ (race discrimination) and the Disability Rights Commission★ (disability discrimination).

The Disability Discrimination Act applies if you have 15 or more employees, but even small firms are due to come under its rules in October 2004. Employees with disabilities must not, without justification, be less favourably treated than other employees for reasons related to their disabilities. Employers may also have to make 'reasonable adjustments' if their premises or working arrangements substantially disadvantage an employee with a disability.

New laws banning discrimination on grounds of age, sexual orientation and religion were under discussion as we went to press.

Health and safety

Health and safety laws place general duties on all people at work – employers, employees and the self-employed, manufacturers, suppliers, designers and importers of materials used at work, and people in control of premises. Regulations specify what must be provided in the way of washrooms, toilets, heat, ventilation and light, somewhere to sit and so on. Other regulations and codes of practice apply to many different work activities.

The requirements to protect health and safety and provide welfare vary considerably depending on the type of work being carried on. You must keep a written risk assessment if you employ five or more people. You should also establish what facilities and safeguards you must provide in matters such as machinery guards, protective clothing, storage and handling of dangerous substances.

Register with the appropriate enforcing authority, which may visit to inspect your premises. For most shops, offices, warehouses, leisure facilities, hotel and catering activities, the enforcing body is the local authority. In the case of manufacturing and most other businesses, it is the Health and Safety Executive (HSE), which runs a Health and Safety Executive Infoline.*

Addresses of local authority enforcement offices can be obtained from district council offices or the local authority liaison officer in the nearest HSE area office. The HSE publishes a range of explanatory and guidance material including *Essentials of Health and Safety at Work* available from HSE Books* and bookshops.

Recording accidents

You must record all accidents at work that involve employees or visitors, though this rule does not apply to some businesses with nine or fewer employees. Serious accidents must be reported on a special form to the relevant enforcing authority, including accidents that result in three or more days off work or at least one day in hospital. Near-miss accidents must also be reported.

First aid

Every place of work should have a first-aid box equipped according to the number of employees on site and the nature of the work. Its contents must be specified and its location known to employees. There should be a correct ratio of trained first-aiders to staff, for example one first-aider for a low-risk office with fewer than 50 employees. All businesses must appoint someone to take control of accidents and look after the first-aid box.

Pay-As-You-Earn

You are the channel by which your employees' Pay-As-You-Earn (PAYE) income tax and National Insurance contributions are transmitted to the Inland Revenue. You also have to pay tax credits to employees who qualify for them. Leaflet CWL3 *Thinking of Taking Someone On?* (available from tax offices) explains the procedure, as does the special Employers' Helpline,* which can arrange for an official to meet you if necessary. Using form CWF3, which is included in the leaflet above, tell your tax office when you take on employees. You will be told which is to be your PAYE office and your employees' PAYE reference numbers. You will also be sent a copy of the *New Employer's Starter Pack*, including the *Employer's Quick Guide to PAYE and NICs*.

You cannot avoid the PAYE system by classing all your staff as self-employed. If the Revenue decides they are actually employees, you may find yourself liable to make back payments of tax and National Insurance after you have paid your staff in full. Leaflet IR56 *Employed or Self-employed?* (available from tax offices) gives guidelines.

PAYE tables tell you how much tax to deduct each week or month according to the individual employee's code. Similarly, other tables tell you how much National Insurance to deduct. You put gross pay and other details on each employee's deductions working sheet, which has a space for each week of the tax year. You must send the deducted tax and National Insurance contributions to the tax Accounts Office once a month or quarterly if you expect the monthly PAYE and National Insurance deductions to be less than £1,000.

An employee who has previously been employed during the tax year should bring you a P45 form, which gives his or her PAYE code number, total pay and total tax deducted so far in the tax year. A new employee without a P45 must sign form P46. You complete it and send it to your PAYE office. Meanwhile you use an emergency code for the employee until you receive the individual code.

You must put details of employee's pay, income tax and National Insurance on form P14 at the end of the tax year. A copy goes to the PAYE tax district along with form P35, an annual statement. Another copy goes to the employee as a form P60.

National Insurance

If their earnings reach the earnings threshold (£4,628 in 2003–4), you have to deduct Class 1 National Insurance contributions from the pay of all employees who are between 16 and the minimum state pension age (currently 65 for a man, 60 for a woman). In addition, you must pay employer's Class 1 National Insurance on earnings above the level of the personal tax allowance. The employer's rate is 11.8 per cent (less if you run a contracted-out pension scheme) on all earnings above the threshold, including the earnings of employees over state pension age who don't pay National Insurance themselves.

If yours is a limited company, you deduct Class 1 National Insurance from your own salary and also pay the employer's contribution of 11.8 per cent.

Chapter 10

Insurance and pensions

Many aspects of running a business can create a need for some kind of insurance. For most kinds, you can find cover although the premiums may sometimes be high. However, premiums paid for any business insurance are expenses that can be set against tax.

A useful introduction to buying insurance is the free booklet *Insurance Advice for Small Businesses*, available from the Association of British Insurers (ABI).* Buying business insurance is complex and rather specialised. Get advice from an insurance broker specialising in commercial insurance, particularly if you need some unusual type of insurance or if you are faced with what seem excessively high premium demands.

There is no easy way to find a good insurance broker, but a personal recommendation is helpful. It is always advisable to see a few brokers before you decide whom to place your business with, and then choose one with whom you'll feel comfortable having a long-term business relationship. Look for a broker who deals with a good range of insurance companies rather than an intermediary who sells products of just one or a small number of insurance companies.

There are degrees of specialisation. Find out what experience and expertise a broker has for small businesses. Look for efficient and knowledgeable staff who are upfront about what they can and cannot offer, who get to know you and your needs, and who have passed exams run by organisations such as the Chartered Insurance Institute.* Insurance advisers are normally paid commission by the companies whose products they sell.

Employer's liability insurance

Employers are legally obliged to cover everyone on the payroll by a minimum of £10 million of employer's liability insurance. You must display a current certificate of insurance at the place of work and keep a copy of the certificate for 40 years. Family businesses with close relations as employees are exempt unless they are trading as limited companies, but it is still sensible to get cover. Family members could sue you for damages and you would probably want them to get compensation from an insurance company if they had a claim.

The employer's liability insurance covers you for claims that might arise if employees suffer physical injury or illness as result of their employment. An employee suing you for damages would need to show that the injury or illness arose from your negligence or that of another employee. This does not mean that you can forget about your legal responsibilities for your employees' health and safety. An insurance company that believes you have failed to meet your legal responsibilities could sue you to recover the cost of any compensation.

Premiums are related to the size of your payroll and will also depend on the risks attached to the jobs. If your employees do only office work, it is likely to cost less than if they work with machinery or shift heavy loads.

The Health and Safety Executive Infoline* publishes a free brochure, *Employer's Liability (Compulsory Insurance) Act 1969: A Guide for Employers*.

Insuring property and equipment

It is sensible to insure for the various disasters that could seriously damage or ruin your business: for example, burglary, fire, flood, subsidence, malicious damage and explosion. Among items to cover against these hazards are the:

- business premises, including site clearance and rebuilding costs
- contents, including fixtures and fittings, industrial plant, computers, tools and other equipment
- stock, including supplies not yet used and goods that have been allocated to customers

- goods in transit such as goods on the way to the customer, to a sub-contractor, to the docks for shipment – whether in your own or someone else's vehicles or by post
- goods on a sub-contractor's premises.

You could take out a separate policy for each kind of risk, but it would be more efficient to have a single insurance policy covering all risks. Many trade associations arrange (or act as agents for) special insurance policies tailored for the needs of the particular trade.

Review and update the amount of cover at regular intervals. Otherwise, you might find a huge discrepancy between the amount you are covered for and what your loss actually amounts to when you need to make a claim.

Working from home

Your existing household insurance may cover your equipment and public liability if you work from home in a small way. But you must tell your insurer that you work from home, or you could find that your cover is invalid. Your insurer is also likely to insist on a special policy once your business equipment rises above a certain value, if your work involves people visiting your home, or if the risk of fire or theft is increased (because you store flammable materials, for example). Several companies now offer policies designed for people who work at home.

Consequential loss insurance

Consequential loss insurance covers losses that would arise if your business were to come to a standstill following a disaster that is covered by basic insurance. Your basic insurance, for example, should cover the cost of rebuilding and re-equipping if your premises burned down. Consequential loss insurance can cover the consequences of a disaster such as wage bills, overheads, lost customers and lost profits.

Public liability insurance

Public liability insurance covers claims by members of the public who have been injured as a result of your (or one of your employees') activities at work: for example, a brick dropped from scaffolding on passers-by.

Product liability insurance

Product liability insurance covers you for claims arising out of faults in something you or your employees have designed, manufactured or serviced: for example, if the folding chair you make collapses under a purchaser or the washing machine you have repaired gives a severe electrical shock. You may be held liable even if you have not been negligent.

Professional indemnity insurance

Professional indemnity insurance covers professionals or other people who provide a service against liability claims resulting from negligent work.

Insurance for car and driver

Third-party motor insurance is compulsory on all the firm's vehicles. It is sensible to insure as well for theft and accidents. If your vehicles are going to be driven by various persons, make sure you get an all-drivers policy.

Consider insuring against the loss of your driving licence if your work involves a lot of driving and your livelihood would be threatened without your licence. The insurance cannot restore your licence, but it can supply the means to hire someone to drive for you.

Make sure that your own private car is also covered for business use if you use it for any business purposes other than driving to and from your place of work.

Insurance if money is lost

A policy to cover lost money can be bought either as a stand-alone policy or as part of a general business-contents policy. It will be valid for loss of money (including cheques and postal orders) from your office, till or house or while in transit: for example, you could be robbed while taking money to the bank. You can also buy insurance to compensate an employee who is injured while being robbed of money.

Firms that hold clients' money, such as travel agents or insurance agents, need an insurance bond to protect them against loss if the business fails. Bonding is compulsory for some types of agency.

Other insurance

There is hardly a calamity for which you cannot insure your business or yourself. Shop-owners, for example, can get insurance to cover plate glass – to board up, repair the damage, compensate for damage or injury by shattered glass, and cover consequential loss of profits.

By becoming a member of the Federation of Small Businesses (FSB),* you are automatically entitled to legal and professional expenses insurance of up to £50,000 for each claim. This gives you some financial protection for various problems, which include Inland Revenue investigations, property disputes, jury service, personal injury and employment disputes, as well as a 24-hour telephone legal advice service. There is also an FSB insurance service should you want to buy other types of business insurance.

Personal insurance

Don't neglect your personal insurance needs. Any illness or accident that takes you out of circulation for any length of time could be damaging – or fatal – to your business.

- Life insurance is a priority if you have dependants who would suffer financial hardship in the event of your death. In addition, you can get cover to pay out if someone with a financial stake in the business were to die. There could be problems if their inheritors decided to sell their stake. Life insurance can provide the money to buy them out.
- Income replacement insurance (sometimes called permanent health insurance) provides a regular income to compensate for your loss of income while you are unable to work through incapacity. It is equivalent to sick pay for employees.
- Private medical insurance is something of a luxury, but gives you some control over the timing of medical treatment. You could hasten treatment that may be affecting your ability to work efficiently or arrange treatment to coincide with a slack business period. You should also consider insuring a partner or employee without whom the business would suffer.

- Key person insurance pays out to the business if the key person is out of action. You can buy life insurance and income replacement for key people.
- Jury service insurance pays out if you or another key person is called for jury service.

Pensions

The basic state pension is small and the National Insurance contributions paid by the self-employed (in contrast to those paid by employees) do not bring any entitlement to the state second pension, which replaced the state earnings-related pension (SERPS) in April 2001. The big mistake of many self-employed people is to wake up one morning at the age of 50 or so and see retirement beginning to loom on the horizon. At that age, it might be too late to start building up a decent pension fund.

Many self-employed people count on selling their business on retirement to produce a retirement income. This means putting all your eggs in one basket and is a high-risk strategy. You may not be able to sell the business, or sell it at the price you want. Many self-employed people – for example, consultants – don't have a business to sell.

It is sensible to make separate investments for retirement, so start a personal pension sooner rather than later and don't underestimate the amount of money you should invest. Even to get a half-decent retirement income, you'll probably need to put aside as much as you can afford. Investing through an official pension arrangement offers tax incentives: contributions (within limits) are tax-free and the money grows in a largely tax-free fund.

It might be worth paying a fee to a specialist for pensions advice rather than go to an adviser who is paid by commission and who might be unduly influenced by this. The Society of Pension Consultants★ and the Association of Consulting Actuaries (ACA)★ can both supply lists of members, and lists of independent financial advisers in your area are available from IFA Promotion★ or the Money Management Register★ of Independent Fee-Based Advisers.

Sole traders and partners

Sole traders and partners (and their employees) can buy a personal pension from a pension provider such as an insurance company. The plan provider invests your money to build up a cash fund. At a set retirement date (which need not be when you actually stop work) you use the fund to provide a regular retirement income for life through the purchase of a pension annuity. Part of the fund can be taken as a tax-free lump sum.

Consider buying a single-premium personal pension rather than one that requires regular contributions. You can vary contributions in line with fluctuating profits in order to help you keep your tax bill to a minimum. Stakeholder pensions are a form of personal pension; they combine flexibility of payment with low charges.

Every few years, consider switching to a different provider so that your retirement is not all riding on the investment skills or continued solvency of just one company.

Company pensions

You have more choice if your business is set up as a company. You can pay into a personal pension or your own employer pension scheme.

Executive pensions are a form of employer pension designed for a small number of members. As employer, you are not constrained by contribution limits on personal pensions. However, the benefits you can take from an executive plan are limited. There is no limit to the overall benefits from a personal pension plan.

Small Self-Administered Schemes (SSASs) are small-employer schemes, usually with fewer than 12 members. They can be a good choice for family-run companies. Specialists such as insurance companies administer them, but you have a wide choice about who will manage your money and how it will be invested. This extra choice requires an extra tier of management charges and these schemes may not be cost-effective unless you have at least £100,000 in the fund.

Some pension arrangements allow you to hold the business's assets in a tax-efficient arrangement. Get specialist advice and weigh up any tax advantages against the downside of risking the fortunes of your pension too closely with the fortunes of your business.

Your pensions choice will be governed by the limits set by the Inland Revenue, on how much you can contribute, the benefits you can draw, the flexibility of the scheme and how the money can be invested.

Chapter 11

Protecting ideas and innovation

Your business may own potentially valuable 'intellectual property', such as an invention, design or logo: consider protecting it against use by others. Alternatively, your ideas might already belong to other people and you could be sued for infringing the rights of others: you may have to withdraw from the market and pay damages.

Patents and other intellectual property rights are easy to ignore. Following the basic rules of intellectual property should help you avoid problems and wasting money. If you are planning to develop a new product, begin by having a patent search made. You may find patent specifications that will prevent you expending time and effort by repeating previous work. Alternatively, you may find an ideal new product for which you can apply for a licence to use in your business.

Intellectual property is the collective term used to refer to the laws that protect:

- copyright
- unregistered design right
- registered designs
- trade marks
- patents.

You may not be granted a patent or registered design if you prematurely disclose information to anyone who is not under a legal obligation of confidentiality. Make sure your employees are fully aware of their legal duty to maintain confidentiality and ask outside contractors to sign an undertaking to keep information confidential.

Copyright

Copyright is a right to prevent others copying what you own. It automatically exists in original 'literary, dramatic, musical or artistic work'. Literary works include computer programs, material published on the Internet, letters, booklets, advertisements, instruction manuals, price lists, business plans and databases. More physical objects such as buildings and sculptures, photographs and drawings also all have copyright.

Any work that is original in the sense that someone has expended skill and effort in its production has copyright. Once the work has been completed the copyright is there. Your business needs only to ensure that it owns the copyright, which it can do by following the basic rules.

- Retain all original works. You could deposit a copy with your bank or solicitor. Alternatively, send a copy to yourself by registered post to prove that the work existed by a particular date. Keep it unopened.
- Ensure that all retained works identify the author and the date made.
- Ensure that your business owns the rights.

Copyright belongs to the author of any piece of work, or to anyone else to whom the author has sold or given copyright, or to a business or other organisation that employed the author if the work was made in the course of employment duties. When you buy in any advertising material, artwork, computer programs and other specialist works, agree at the outset and in writing who is to own any copyright.

Be prepared to enforce your copyright if necessary. A competitor, for example, may issue a leaflet that is the same or similar to one of your own. In this case, you can take legal action to have the competitor's leaflet withdrawn and all copies destroyed. You may also be able to claim damages. However, try to discourage copying by putting a copyright notice on original works made available to the public. Such a notice is the word 'copyright' or the symbol ©, followed by the year of publication and the copyright owner's name.

For work originating in the UK and most continental European countries, copyright in a literary, dramatic, musical or artistic work (including photographs) lasts until 70 years after the death of the author. Sound recordings, broadcasts and cable programmes are protected for 50 years, and published editions for 25 years. In other countries, the term of protection is that given by the country of origin and may be shorter.

Unregistered design right

Manufactured products were also protected by copyright until 1 August 1989, since when they have been protected by the unregistered design right. This gives limited protection for manufactured goods: for example, furniture, engineering products, tools, containers, clothing, toys and models, office equipment, packaging, jewellery, stationery, and consumer goods in general. Unregistered design right is similar to copyright, and it arises automatically to prevent copying or imitation. In most cases, it lasts for only 10 years from the date a product is first marketed. You can enforce your unregistered design right if necessary, providing you have retained the original drawings or the first prototype of the new product.

Registered designs

A registered design can give better protection than unregistered design right because it lasts up to 25 years (not 10). The owner of a registered design can stop anyone in the UK making, selling, using or importing articles with the same or similar design without having to prove that the design has been copied. To obtain a registered design it is necessary to go through an application process so that the Designs Registry at the Patent Office,★ acting on behalf of the public, can satisfy itself that the application meets the necessary criteria. Your application should be accompanied by drawings or photographs showing the article.

The first requirement of a registered design is that it is new. The article must look different from previous designs and must not have already been sold or otherwise disclosed in the UK. Generally, you must apply before the product goes on the market. But you can register a valid design after there has been some disclosure of it if fewer than 50 articles have been produced and there have been no commercial dealings in the articles.

The second requirement is that an article should be designed specifically to have an aesthetic appearance or otherwise appeal to the eye. You can, for example, register the design of office equipment and furniture that is sold on appearance, but you cannot register the design of solely functional articles such as fuses.

The examiner of the Designs Registry will consider the application and issue a certificate of registration if there are no objections. Be prepared to persuade the examiner by argument or amendment that you can overcome any objections.

Articles such as works of sculpture, wall plaques and medals, and printed matter (for example, calendars, greetings cards, maps and playing cards) are specifically excluded from registration.

Trade marks

A trade mark is a word or symbol that distinguishes the goods and services of one business from those of others. It applies to the origin of goods and services rather than their nature. A book, for example, carrying the trade mark Michelin™, tells you that the French tyre company has originated or is in some way connected with the book, not that the book is made of rubber or about rubber products. A strong brand is extremely valuable and acquires reputation and goodwill.

It is possible to acquire rights to a mark automatically, simply by using it. Where your use is so substantial that a considerable reputation has been built up, competitors can be stopped from imitating that mark by an action of 'passing off'. However, a strong brand is extremely valuable and ought to be protected even before goodwill and reputation have been accrued. This can be done by registering the mark. You have to register the mark in respect of specific goods or services, though; you cannot register a blanket right to it.

Apply to the Trade Marks Registry at the Patent Office.★ A trade mark examiner will consider the application and ensure that the proposed mark does not conflict with any existing registrations or applications in the pipeline. An application helps prevent competitors registering similar marks and serves as a warning to others of your rights in the mark.

You can ensure that a mark or brand you want to use does not infringe any existing rights by carrying out trade-mark searches.

Patents

Patents are the most powerful of all intellectual property rights. Like a registered design, a patent gives you a monopoly but one that protects much more than the visual appearance of an article. It can also defend the basic concept of a project. It is suitable for 'inventions' – things that can be made or used in any kind of industry: for example, machines, methods of making and testing products and processes. Some things are specifically excluded from patent protection, including discoveries, literary works, rules for playing games, methods of doing business and computer programs.

Many businesses don't apply for patents because they are complex and expensive and they believe competitors will easily be able to get round the patent by making minor changes. But patents are extremely powerful business tools, and the cost of acquiring a patent in the UK, which gives the owner an absolute monopoly for 20 years, can be less than the expense of putting a quarter-page advertisement in a national newspaper.

To be granted a patent it is necessary to go through an application procedure so that the Patent Office★ can establish that the necessary criteria have been met. This involves filing at the Patent Office a request for a patent specification. This specification has to include a technical description, with enough detail to enable someone to make or perform the invention. This means that the published patent specifications are an extremely valuable source of technical information. Your patent specification must also include at least one 'claim' – a statement setting out the scope of protection you want.

An examiner in the Patent Office will search through earlier patent documents to test the novelty of the proposal. Then your application is published to alert the public to its existence and to its contents. You then have to persuade the examiner by argument or amendment that you can overcome any objections. Not all patent applications are successful.

An invention must be both new and non-obvious. An invention is new if it has not been made available in any way, to anyone, anywhere in the world at the time you apply for a patent. Keep details of all projects confidential (see above) until you have decided whether or not to apply for a patent. An invention is obvious if a person skilled in the field would think the invention trivial or an inevitable development of what is already known. However, being obvious is not the same as being simple. Many patents are granted for small and simple improvements: for example, to fixings, packaging and other everyday products.

Intellectual property outside the UK

Intellectual property is international. Most countries provide rights that are very similar to those of the UK. Copyright is recognised in most countries and you can generally take action against plagiarists around the world, citing copyright that has originated in the UK.

For registered designs and registered trade marks, you can make a separate application in each country where you want protection. You don't have to do this at the same time as you apply in the UK. Under an international agreement, you can apply to register design and trade marks abroad and have them backdated to the date of the first UK application if you apply within six months of the first UK application.

You may not need to make separate applications in each country.

- A European Union system allows you to register trade marks with the Office for Harmonisation in the Internal Market (Trade Marks and Designs).* It protects you anywhere in the European Union. However, if you are selling to just one or two member countries, it may be cheaper and simpler to register separately in the UK and in each of the other countries.
- The European Patent Convention allows a single European patent to cover up to 20 or so European countries, including the UK. The system is expensive but a boon to companies needing extensive protection in Europe.
- The international system under the Patent Co-operative Treaty (PCT) allows a single application for nearly 100 countries worldwide.

Getting help

It is generally advisable to seek professional help from a Chartered Patent Agent (CPA) for any intellectual property issues. Look in *Yellow Pages* under 'Patent Agents' or 'Trade Mark Agents' or in a regional directory of the Chartered Institute of Patent Agents★. This publishes free booklets on patents, trade and service marks, and industrial designs. Many patent agents offer free preliminary advice under, for example, the Chartered Institute's scheme 'Patent Agents for Innovation'.

Patent agents can apply for any of the intellectual property rights, make searches to see if ideas are new, check your freedom to use new ideas and innovations, and advise and act if things go wrong. They can assist on agreements, licensing and other commercial dealings with such rights.

The UK Patent Office★ publishes free information on obtaining patents, designs and trade marks. The Patent Office Search and Advisory Service★ can carry out searches for you for a fee. Alternatively, do your own searches through:

- British Library Science Reference and Information Service★, which has a comprehensive collection of British and foreign patents
- patent collections that are held in patent libraries in regional centres
- your local Business Link★ (or the alternatives outside England) as it may be able to tell you what is available in your area
- the Internet via the Patent Office website.

Chapter 12

Finding business premises

The kind of space in which you need to work, and where it is situated, will depend largely on whether you offer a service, manufacture goods or sell them (see Chapter 14). Here are some questions to consider when looking for convenient premises. Are they:

- easy for you to reach, in terms of time, distance and traffic?
- convenient for employees to get to? Are they served by public transport? Will employees be able to park their cars?
- in an area where you will be able easily to hire at reasonable rates the sort of employees you will need?
- attractive in themselves and in an area that is appealing to employees in terms of amenities such as shops and cafes? Good premises in an sought-after area may make it easier to recruit and retain staff
- impressive to potential customers if they are likely to visit your business?
- near a good road network or ports or airports, if these things have a bearing on the type of business you run? You will want to minimise the costs of getting supplies delivered and of delivering your own end product
- near your customers if you run a service business?
- in an area where your business can benefit from central and local government grants and other incentives?

Subletting premises

If you need only a modest amount of space, you may be able to find an existing business that has spare capacity and is glad to reduce its overheads by subletting to you. Look for a similar but not competing type of business; associating with them could even result in a partnership.

Health and safety

Wherever you find suitable premises, remember that offices, shops, factories and many other types of commercial accommodation have to comply with regulations about the safety of staff and facilities for them. Make sure that your prospective premises either accord with the regulations or are capable of being modified to comply with them. You can get free leaflets from the Health and Safety Executive's publications section HSE Books* and information from the Health and Safety Executive Infoline* or your local authority's planning department.

Fire prevention

You have legal obligations to assess fire risk and take the necessary precautions even if you have only one employee. You may have to install fire-detection equipment and alarms, fire-fighting equipment, fire escapes, emergency doors and emergency lighting. Premises require a fire certificate if they are used as a place of work such as a shop, factory or office where more than 20 people are employed, or more than 10 people elsewhere than on the ground floor, or if explosives or highly flammable substances are stored there.

Consult the local fire safety officer before you sign for any premises. If your business requires the installation of new fire escapes, fire doors or new flooring, the premises may be beyond your budget. You may be refused insurance or other permission required for your business if you fail to comply with a fire safety officer's directions. You could be prosecuted, and in the worst case your business could even be closed down.

If you are looking at previously occupied premises, find out whether there is a current fire certificate and, if so, whether it will cover your operations. If your occupancy constitutes a change of conditions because of structural alterations or a change of use or in the number of persons working there, you will need a new certificate. A local fire safety officer will have to inspect the premises and check that all necessary precautions have been taken.

Access for disabled people

Disability discrimination laws place duties on those providing goods, facilities and service not to discriminate against disabled people. As a service provider, you must take reasonable steps to:

- change any practices that make it impossible or unreasonably difficult for disabled people to use your service
- provide auxiliary aids or services to make it easier for disabled people to use your service
- overcome any physical features that make it impossible or unreasonably difficult for disabled people to use a service by providing the service by a reasonable alternative method.

From 2004, you will have to take reasonable steps to change (or provide sensible means of avoiding) physical features that make it difficult or impossible for disabled people to use your service. It may make financial sense to carry out alterations when you acquire new premises rather than undertake further works in 2004. Make sure a lease allows you to make alterations to comply with the law: the landlord cannot refuse permission without good reason.

You can get leaflets with more details from the Disability Discrimination Act Helpline.★ The Centre for Accessible Environments★ can provide design guidance and also (for a charge) audit your premises.

Planning permission

Make sure that the premises you choose already have the appropriate planning permission. If they do not, you will have to apply to the local authority's planning department for permission to make alterations or change the use of the premises. This can take months and is an extra expense. If you intend to start from a green-field site and build on it, planning permission will take much longer, and is only one of the obstacles to be overcome.

A free booklet, *Planning Permission: A Guide for Business*, is available from the Department of Transport.★

Rate relief and concessions

If you are not tied to any one area and can set up anywhere, you may be better off in an assisted area, where you may sometimes get subsidised accommodation.

English Partnerships★ is a government agency with a remit to release the potential of derelict and vacant land throughout England. It can offer various types of support, such as loan guarantees. In some areas it undertakes the development itself, making commercial and industrial premises available for rent.

Many local authorities are prepared to give initial rate relief to new businesses and those relocating into the area. Get in touch with the planning department or the economic unit of your local authority about these or other concessions.

Premises for a service industry

If you provide a service – for example, as a builder, decorator or plumber – much of your work may be carried out in your customers' premises. Initially, you may need only some space at home to do the paperwork, and perhaps a shed or garage for storing tools. But if your business grows and you employ staff, you may eventually want separate business premises: for example, an office to deal with enquiries, estimates and paperwork; larger storage space; and parking for your vans. Plan ahead for this possibility.

Your service business may be a consultancy or agency requiring little or no equipment or storage space. The physical location of your office may not be crucial to your success. If so, using part of your home for business use could be the best option.

Serviced offices

Serviced offices are available for a weekly or monthly charge, and the names of organisations running them can be found in *Yellow Pages* under 'Office Rental'. Such offices may be convenient and, depending on the location, allow you to present an up-market image. They can offer: use of a full-time office or just an occasional meeting room; telephone-answering services; voice mail; fax services; Internet access; and post forwarding. They can provide a base in other countries for people who do business overseas.

When you have found a possible serviced office, check the terms and conditions thoroughly. How long are you committed for? What is the landlord legally committed to provide? What comeback is there if the services supplied are not up to scratch? Contact other users of the service to see what their experience has been. Compare a serviced office with the cost and convenience of putting together your own package. Answerphone services and voice mail are available from phone companies, and fax machines are relatively cheap to buy. If you don't need a full-time office, you could rent conference rooms in a local hotel for meetings as and when you need them.

Working from home

Working from home has an advantage for a very small or new business: you save on rent, rates, the cost of the utilities and the expense of travelling to and from work. You can also save on staff, if a family member answers the door and the phone and perhaps helps with general administration. But consider the following points.

- Some house deeds prohibit use for business purposes and contain restrictive covenants that could be enforced.
- You may need planning permission from the local authority: for example, if your home needs to be altered by the addition or modification of a room or shed or the type of business activity requires it. You may get planning permission qualified by some conditions relating to hours of work, or callers at the house. You have the right to appeal but will have to look elsewhere for premises if you lose an appeal.
- You may have to pay business-rate utility and other charges if you carry on a business from residential premises.
- You should inform the company that insures your home if you use it for business. Otherwise, you may invalidate your buildings and contents insurance – even against disasters, such as a burst water pipe, that are totally unrelated to your use of the home for business purposes. And you should tell your insurer about specific business-related matters that may increase the risk: for example, if you have customers entering your home, or keep expensive business-related equipment in the home, or store combustible materials.

- You may also want to check that your mortgage lender has no objections.
- If you claim a proportion of the expenses of running your home as a business expense, you risk a capital gains tax on the same proportion of the gains when you eventually sell it. A small gain may well fall within your exempt allowance for the year in which you sell, but check the position with your accountant.

Premises for a manufacturing business

Working from home is rarely an option for a manufacturing business unless you are a craftsperson working single-handed and in a very small business. Apart from the probable lack of workshop space, you may well run into opposition from the local authority or neighbours. It is unlikely that you could carry on a manufacturing business clandestinely or that you would get permission to do so in residential premises.

A manufacturing business must satisfy zoning regulations for light and heavy industry, because it may create noise, smoke, fumes, industrial waste that must be disposed of and other sorts of environmental pollution; or it may increase the risk of fire.

Finding workshop space

Before you start searching, draw up a list defining your exact requirements. These may include access to all the mains services, warehousing space, office space, reception area, a room and amenities for the employees, parking space, room for lorries to load and unload and so on. Consider getting premises big enough for your business to expand without the need to move in a year or two.

Spread your search as wide as possible so that you get the most suitable premises currently available.

- Your local Business Link★ (or the alternatives outside England) can advise on what's available in your area.
- Members of the local small business club can provide good information and advice.
- Local authorities cater for the very small business by building small units that are shells and sometimes only 50 square metres (about the size of a double garage). The rents are not necessarily

low, but an authority keen to promote employment may subsidise them or offer other incentives.

- Local authorities keep a register of vacant industrial property and can extract from it a list of suitable premises.
- Local estate agents may deal in commercial and industrial property. Once you have given them your details and requirements, phone them at intervals to remind them of your existence. Low-cost, low-rental premises have little value to an agent because they bring in a low fee and you may be forgotten. Also, keep an eye out for very small and cheap premises in the centre of town that do not always reach the estate agents' lists.
- Classified advertisements in the local press.

Buying a lease

Some business premises are sold freehold but the majority are available only on lease. For a new business, a lease has the advantages of being relatively cheap to acquire and of not necessarily needing a long-term commitment. In purchasing leasehold premises you usually buy the assignment of an existing lease that was negotiated between the landlord and the original tenant.

A business lease is a technical document and regulates your legal relationship with the landlord, so you should employ a solicitor experienced in this field. Your Business Link* (or the alternatives outside England) may know of specialist solicitors in your area. When you receive the draft lease, read it and any attached schedules carefully. Mark (in pencil and on a copy) the points that are important to you and things you do not understand. Draw your solicitor's attention to points that concern you. Your solicitor may not understand the nitty-gritty of how your particular business works and what may be important in the lease.

You are more likely to come across a new lease if someone selling a business is the freeholder and wants to remain landlord. Landlords will naturally bias leases in their favour, but there may be room for negotiation. Take the trouble to get the terms of the lease right. Once agreed and signed, it may be difficult and expensive to change.

Here is a brief guide to some of the issues and the questions you should ask.

Rent

The rent will probably be due in instalments throughout the year. What is the current rent? When and how often is it reviewed? Will the new rent be linked to the retail prices index (unlikely) or be determined by reference to rentals of comparable premises? What other payments will be due to the landlord: for example, insurance and service charges?

Cost of purchase

A tenant selling an existing lease may ask for a premium (a capital sum) from an incoming tenant. This will be determined by market forces: for example, a lease with a low rent or for a particularly attractive site might attract a considerable premium, while one with little time to run may be difficult to sell and so command little or no premium. If the commercial property market is in the doldrums, a tenant keen to sell may even pay a buyer a 'reverse premium' to take over the lease.

It is unusual to pay a premium for a new lease but a tenant may have to pay the landlord's legal costs for granting the lease. If a new lease requires you to spend money on fitting out the premises, you may be able negotiate a rent-free period as recompense.

Length of lease

When does the lease come to an end? Does the landlord have the right to end it early? You will minimise your responsibilities by acquiring premises on as short a lease as possible. But what are your rights if you want to stay on at the premises once the lease has come to an end?

Ideally your lease would give you an optional right to a new lease, but this is not always so. A tenant of business premises has a right to apply to the court for the grant of a new lease (with some minor exceptions) but the landlord may have grounds for objecting. A tenant cannot be sure of getting a new lease against a landlord's opposition. In practice, most disputes are settled by negotiation. A free leaflet, *Business Leases and Security of Tenure*, is available from the Department of Transport.★

Getting rid of the lease

Circumstances may force you to sublet, surrender a lease early or sell it to a new tenant. Check the lease particularly carefully for your rights in these situations. The landlord will want to vet any prospective tenants. A landlord cannot unreasonably refuse to allow a lease to be assigned to a new tenant, but can impose financial and other preconditions that have to be met. A particularly nasty precondition to beware of is that you could remain liable for any rent unpaid by future tenants.

Permitted use

Does the lease allow you to use the premises for your present and future business use? Can the landlord be required to consent to a change in permitted use? Will limitations on permitted uses affect the marketability of the lease when you want to sell it?

Repairs

Who is responsible for repairs? If it's the tenant, is there any cap on the amount you might have to pay? Ensure that there is a full description of the premises, to establish the limits of liability for repairs. Are you liable for the foundations? The roof? The load-bearing walls? Money spent on repairing someone else's property is money you will not see again.

Unless the landlord is fully responsible for repairs and their cost, you should have a full structural survey of the premises before you buy. If the survey sounds expensive, negotiate the fee and scope of the survey. You do not want a lengthy catalogue listing features that you can see for yourself, nor a full unlimited guarantee on which you could sue if the surveyor missed anything. You want a realistic guide to the value of the property and a list of repairs needed immediately, repairs that you can risk leaving for a while, and what is unimportant structurally. Ask the surveyor to confirm information given by the landlord, such as the amount of business rates.

Alterations

What kind of alterations can be carried out without permission from the landlord? Does the landlord's permission have to be obtained for business signs? If the property needs to be refurbished at your expense you will increase its value to the owner, so you may be able to negotiate a cheaper rent.

Services

Check that there will be no difficulties with the mains services, that there will be enough electric power, water, gas, adequate drainage, and no difficulties about phone services.

Chapter 13

Using computers

Computers are invaluable in almost any business: they can increase efficiency, save time and help keep things under control. They can enable even the smallest business to present a slick, efficient and professional image to the outside world: to suppliers, customers, central and local government and any other group or organisation a business needs to impress.

Computers – also called 'information technology' or 'IT' – can be used for:

- developing a business plan
- costings, estimates and quotations
- invoices and statements
- book-keeping and preparation of accounts
- financial projections, including forecasting of cash flow and profit and loss
- stock control
- standard letters to suppliers and customers
- advertising and promotional literature
- databases (e.g., of customer details and of all historic information connected with the business)
- payroll management, including PAYE and National Insurance contributions
- filing tax and VAT returns
- sending and receiving faxes
- as an answerphone
- emails to communicate instantly
- sending and receiving various different types of document
- buying from suppliers
- selling your product or service through your own website
- surfing the Internet for ideas, information and news.

But before you buy the latest computer (and various optional accessories), you need to justify its cost against the extent to which you will use it. What in practice will you do with it? A computer can be all-singing and dancing – the difficult bit is deciding which skills to master to get the maximum benefit from it. There is a danger that a computer can become an expensive and possibly little-used toy or, worse, a white elephant. Small, single-person, uncomplicated businesses can still be successful without a computer.

Getting computer advice

Take your time in choosing a computer system. Ultimately, you want one that does everything you need it to do and that you and any employees will find reasonably straightforward to operate. Don't be tempted to buy an expensive system with lots of programs you may never have time to run. But don't necessarily go for the cheapest option – you may find it unnecessarily limits what you can do.

Consider paying for the services of a computer (or IT) consultant, whose advice would be particularly useful if your business employs a number of staff operating computers intensively. You will need to be fairly precise in describing your requirements to a consultant. Other sources of information about computers include:

- specialist computer and business magazines
- computer books – find one that is appropriate to your level of expertise
- specialist computer shops (and possibly chain stores that sell computers – but they tend to aim for the home computer market and staff may have only rudimentary expertise)
- the Internet – where many computer companies have their own websites detailing their range of products
- computer exhibitions
- friends who work with computers
- other small businesses that are computerised
- computer courses
- the National Computing Centre*
- the Federation of Information Systems Centres – an independent government-established body, with centres located

throughout the UK (details from your local Business Link* or the alternatives outside England).

What you need

The cost of a business computer can start at about £500 but, in practice, a very small business will probably spend about £1,000 on a reasonably up-to-date computer that provides substantial internal storage space for programs and information. The cost of the whole system will depend on your requirements: £2,500 may be considered a likely figure for all but the smallest businesses. It's a lot of money but the price of computer equipment has been falling while its quality and power have been improving. In larger businesses, a well-utilised computer enables you to run your business with fewer staff than would otherwise be required.

The computer is likely to be sold as a package with built-in modem (for access to phone lines) and a screen. In order to process and reproduce the information that you feed in, you also need:

- a printer – anything from a cheap ink-jet printer that prints in black and white (or colour) to a more expensive laser printer, with a top-of-the-range colour printer producing print-shop-quality results
- a scanner (to copy images and documents on to the computer and screen)
- stationery and consumables – floppy disks, paper and other printer supplies
- the program or programs that you intend to run on the computer.

Computer hardware

Computer hardware is the machinery in the system – computer, modem, screen, printer and scanner. Most computers are 'personal computers' (PCs), made by a range of different companies. Other computer systems include the Apple Mac, developed independently of the PC and with its own set of programs. It has devoted fans who extol its virtues over PCs and is especially popular in businesses such as publishing, which produce a lot of graphics.

Some computer companies have a reputation for better reliability than others, but what is as important as brand is the technical specifications. These vary enormously, but three key factors affect your choice and the price you pay.

- Speed – this depends on the all-important processor chip, which is given a rating in megahertz (MHz). The higher this number, the faster the computer will work. Speed also depends on a number of other factors.
- Working memory (RAM) – too little working memory can slow a computer to a crawl. Working memory is shown in megabytes (Mb).
- Filing space – filing space for software and your own information is provided by a 'hard disk' and measured in gigabytes (Gb).

You can connect computers in your business in a network so that they share information and extras such as printers and scanners. You can also buy ready-made systems that come with all the extra hardware and software you need. A computer consultant can advise on this.

Computer software

There are two types of software (or computer programs).

- Operating software manages the computer's own resources. Microsoft Windows for PCs is the most commonly used. Apple Macs have their own operating system.
- Application software does specific jobs (e.g. word-processing, accounting, financial planning, tax, stock control, databases).

When you buy a computer you are likely to be supplied with an integrated package providing word-processing, database, spreadsheet and communications functions. But there is plenty of off-the-shelf software on which you can spend your money, too. Some of it may be more suited to your business needs than that supplied with your computer. Look for tried-and-tested software that could be suitable for your business, and find out how any other businesses use the same software. Try to arrange to test existing software before committing yourself.

In addition to off-the-shelf software, you can get software programs written specifically for your business. Such tailor-made programs are generally quite expensive. They might well be more suitable later, when your business has grown and you have a clearer idea of what you want your computer system to do. Paying for tailor-made software could then become a sound investment to increase the efficiency or scope of your business.

Maintenance contracts

When you buy the computer, you may be able to buy a warranty lasting from one to three years. Find out whether it includes visits by engineers when you have a problem. Otherwise consider setting up a maintenance contract, so your computer will be repaired as soon as possible if it breaks down. You may opt for a contract that provides a replacement until your machine is back in running order. Such a contract can also provide troubleshooting for computer viruses and other problems and, possibly, software updates.

An annual maintenance contract typically costs up to 15 per cent of the cost of the computer or software to which it relates. Call-out fees for the engineers are often charged as well – in which case your contract offers little more than the availability of specialised help. But without it you might be in dire straits.

Training

Those new to computers – and even those with some experience – are unlikely to get the best from them by wading through the copious, thick instruction manuals that come with every piece of hardware and software. You need to arrange training for whoever is to use the computer system, including yourself – especially if you are a one-person business. If the computer is wanted for management purposes (for example, to get information on the accounts), you as owner of the business ought to have at least a nodding acquaintance with the software used.

Even though it absorbs both time and money, training could prove a good investment. The cost of training – and of getting your computer up and running – may be part of the 'package' cost if you are buying an entire system for a specialised purpose.

Computer courses vary from brief introductions to longer ones covering advanced subjects. They are often advertised in computer and business magazines. Your local university, college or adult education centre may run classes, too.

Backing up data

Once a computer is turned off, all the information in the working memory is lost. To keep your work, you will need to save it. In addition it is sensible to keep back-up copies of all files and software on your computer. In the worst case, losing everything could be disastrous for a business. You should make sure that back-ups are performed regularly – at least once a day for important work – and that you keep back-up copies of your software in a safe place away from the computer.

Your computer will have a built-in hard disk, which stores information when you are not working on it. There will probably also be a CD-ROM slot and possibly a floppy disk slot, which can both be used to add new software to the computer and to keep back-up (safety) copies of work and of the software you use.

If you need to back up a lot of information you should consider getting special hardware to help you. Options include built-in or removable drives such as Zip and Jaz drives and CD writers, which store information on special blank CDs. CD and DVD-RAM systems work rather like rewritable CDs but with a higher capacity.

Viruses

Viruses are programs that are designed vindictively to destroy the information on your computer. You can accidentally become infected when connected to the Internet, and especially by downloading a contaminated email or attachment, or by loading an infected file on to your computer. You should be able to combat computer viruses with anti-virus software, which will also check the health of your system, but you must update it regularly (at least once a week) to protect your computer from attack. Don't skimp when it comes to investing in a good anti-virus program. Be wary of introducing games or other non-business software to your computer – and especially of opening odd-looking e-mails, particularly junk emails from people you have never had dealings with or even heard of.

Chapter 14

Being a retailer

Large retail chain stores tend to dominate town centres, shopping malls and retail parks. Yet among the familiar fascias are those of smaller businesses with just the one shop, or perhaps one or two branches. In villages, suburban shopping parades and tourist areas, individual businesses may be in the majority.

Big retail businesses have many advantages over smaller outlets. They can, for example, buy cheaply in bulk and display a wide range of goods on their vast floor spaces. This gives them the edge on price and variety. And they have another key asset – brand recognition. If you are in a strange town and fancy a pizza, would you patronise an Italian restaurant that you can't quite make up your mind about or visit a branch of a tried-and-tested brand-name pizza chain? Even if you are prepared to be adventurous by sampling the Italian restaurant, many other consumers would prefer to play safe and go to the big chain.

Small shops have to fight the giants for a share of the customers' spending power, by finding a way of turning their small size to advantage. They can do this, for example, by selling:

- products from local suppliers
- something the big stores don't offer (e.g., fish and chips or antiques)
- products from small manufacturers that are distinctively different from mass-produced goods sold by the big stores
- to particular local communities the big stores don't cater for (e.g., a Caribbean food store or a Bollywood video rental business)
- from locations where the big stores don't go (e.g., a stationers selling computer accessories might have a ready market in a small high street or suburban shopping parade).

Small shops can also offer expert advice: for example, on decorating and home improvements or flowers and plants, where the typical big store sales assistant may not know.

In many areas, late opening hours for small shops is no longer the advantage it used to be. Although big stores have extended their opening hours over recent years, shops with an internal sales area of more than 280 square metres are restricted to opening a maximum of six hours on a Sunday and cannot open on Easter Sunday or Christmas Day if it falls on a Sunday. Motor and cycle supply shops, off-licences, pharmacists and farm shops as well as those at airports, railway stations, petrol stations and service areas can open on Sunday whatever their size.

Selling from a stall

Market stalls and country fairs may provide a useful outlet for a small business making a slow, cautious start at selling. They are particularly suited to craft goods. The local authority will be able to tell you where and when fairs are held in the district, and who to contact about renting a stall, either permanently or by the day.

Exhibiting at a local craft fair could be a good way of launching a product. Some craft associations will arrange to exhibit members' work. The *Showman's Directory*★ will give you a list of 'non-craft' events throughout the country, which might be of use in finding appropriate locations for selling or publicity; it will also tell you where to hire marquees and other equipment.

Popular retail businesses

For people hoping to become their own boss, there are some retail businesses that have an enduring appeal. Many of these seem to require no special training yet bring you in contact with things that are generally associated with pleasure: alcoholic drink, food, magazines, sweets, books, clothes. There is a huge range of retail businesses. *The Retail Directory*★ gives detailed information on retail activities across the country, including turnover for major product ranges and surveys of major outlets in many larger British towns and cities.

Do your research, preparation and planning thoroughly. Running a shop may seem like something anyone can do but you must be realistic about the problems. Many shops are open early in the morning, late at night, on Sundays and bank holidays – and the owners must still to find time to do the paperwork.

Ideally, you should have experience of the retail trade in general and the specific type of retail business that interests you. If, for example, you'd like to run a book shop, try and get a job in one to learn how the book trade works. If you can't afford to give up your salary just yet, see whether you can get work in the evenings or at weekends.

Local general shop

A thriving, well-run corner shop can provide a regular source of income and become a saleable asset, but consider the financial investment needed before you are likely to recoup significant profits. Start-up costs can be considerable. In addition to the expense of any shop refurbishment, you may have to meet the cost of installing equipment for stocking chilled and frozen foods and display units. If you decide to buy premises you need to consider whether you can cut expenses by living above the shop. Leasing will also require substantial financial investment.

When deciding whether to open a local general shop, consider the following points.

- Many general shops are family businesses, which can work well if all the members are committed to the enterprise but can create problems when the business runs into difficulty or individuals have health problems.
- You will probably need to be a grocer, newsagent, off-licence and confectioner rolled into one. And you'll have to compete with the growing trend for the big supermarket chains to open small local branches.
- You'll have to offer convenience, a personal service and ease of access to people in your locality. Lottery tickets and community notice boards can help bring in customers and hopefully these will lead to small, unplanned purchases. A friendly, helpful manner will generate goodwill and customer loyalty and forge links in the community.
- There are regulations with which you need to comply if you use children for newspaper rounds or as additional shop assistants.

Local authorities provide guidelines on employing young people, and these need to be strictly adhered to.

- The village shop and inner-city general store are increasingly seen by planners and local authorities as providing a useful social amenity and focal point for community life, especially if there is no similar outlet. A business may therefore be eligible for grants and additional support in some areas. The Countryside Agency★ has regional offices that can advise you on this, and urban-regeneration projects can provide information on funds available for small businesses in deprived regions. Your local authority will know what is available in your area.

Clothes shop

Most small clothes shops concentrate on a niche market, such as children's clothes, sportswear, outdoor clothing or clothes for the larger customer. Clothes shopping can be a lifestyle experience, so make sure that you choose shop décor and fittings with care. You will need changing facilities, mirrors, good lighting, possibly a small sitting area, background music and attractive carrier bags. Below are a few thoughts and tips on running a clothes shop.

- The fashion industry is fickle and today's fast-selling outfit can be out of date very quickly. Select the clothes you sell carefully. You need to consider how much stock to buy, store and display. The season before you plan to open, visit major wholesalers and production outlets as well as major trade events: for example, The Clothes Show. Try to monitor trends and see how they sell over the following months. Assess forecasts in the leading retail journals (such as *Drapers Record* and *Women's Wear Buyer*) and in the fashion pages of national newspapers and fashion magazines that reflect your chosen customer profile.
- Branded accessories and designer labels are popular with a wide age range of customers and can attract buyers who are looking for something special. The clothes trade is partly about image and creating confidence in your clients.
- Electronic Point-of-Sale (EPoS) systems tag clothes and allow easy re-ordering at source. This can avoid carrying a large volume of stock and ease potential cash-flow problems.

- Take out advertisements announcing the shop's opening in the local press. Arrange a launch party, and follow up with other carefully planned events to boost your business's profile – it will pay to build up a list of customers' names and addresses.
- Small seasonal fashion shows, private promotional viewings, seasonal discounts and mail shots announcing new lines and a personal service will all help maintain customer loyalty.
- Shop-window displays are crucial in catching the eye of many shoppers. You should consider investing in mannequins. There is an increasing range of these available (the trade press has details) and they can display clothes to best advantage. However, creative displays can often be accomplished with just skilful draping, pins, tape and ingenious props.

Book shop

Running a book shop may sound like an idyllic life, but enthusiasm for books is not enough to become a successful independent book-seller. An understanding of retailing in general is essential, as well as a good knowledge of the way the book trade works, in order to compete with the ever-increasing number of chain and multiple book shops.

- Many independent book shops are successful because they provide a good service, or devote themselves to specialising in a particular area (such as children's books, medical texts, history, cinema). Others widen their market by offering a mail order or Internet service in their specialist area.
- As well as selling books, you can attract customers by offering cards and gifts and letting space to a café. You may counter the disadvantage of having a small stock by building a reputation for swift and efficient ordering.
- Publishers offer the retailer set discount rates, which are typically 35 per cent but vary from publisher to publisher, and from book to book. Net profit in bookselling is notoriously low. Larger orders carry larger discounts, but it is a gamble to buy a large number of copies on the chance of a potential best-seller. No bookseller can stock more than a fraction of the hundreds of thousands of titles in print. Careful stock control is vital, as dog-eared books are unlikely to be saleable.

- The Booksellers Association of Great Britain and Ireland★ offers advice, information and training. It publishes a free leaflet, *Starting a Book Shop*, aimed at new entrants to the trade who need to know about the workings of a book shop. It also sells the book *The Complete Guide to Starting and Running a Book Shop*. It negotiates preferential rates for members on many essential services, such as insurance, credit cards and parcel delivery. Joining allows you to participate in the book tokens scheme and the Booksellers Clearing House, a central clearing facility that enables booksellers to pay a large number of publishers' monthly accounts in one single payment.

Café/Bar

Creating the right atmosphere is often the key to running a popular café or bar. When they cross the threshold, most customers are buying more than a cup of coffee or a cocktail. If you can identify and provide what they are looking for, you will be on to a winner. Think about similar places that you have enjoyed. Décor, music, style of food and drink and the floor plan will all play their part in making customers feel comfortable, relaxed and encouraged to return.

- A theme will help give your business an identity and help market and advertise your premises. It may also help you focus on the type of customers you want to attract: for example, a nautical interior may appeal to holidaymakers near a marina; city-centre shoppers may appreciate a continental-style café.
- If you want to provide live entertainment you will need a Performing Rights Society★ licence, and if you plan playing recorded music you must obtain a licence from Phonographic Performance Ltd.★
- It is worth taking into account disturbance levels and possible aggravated neighbours if you plan to keep your premises open late in the evening. Many local authorities have an officer who can give advice.
- You will need to keep the place clean and well maintained and abide by environmental health regulations (both the kitchen and toilet areas must meet stipulated standards).

- Staff must be over 18 years of age if you are selling alcohol, and it helps if they have a pleasant, efficient manner and patience. Effective supervision can make all the difference in ensuring customers and staff remain happy.

- A range of courses is available to help meet catering and customer service standards. The British Institute of Innkeeping* encourages high standards and runs accredited courses around the country. The Royal Institute of Public Health and Hygiene* advises on details of training courses for those involved in handling food, and gives general advice on food hygiene.

- You need to decide how much food preparation you want to do on the premises and how much you prefer to buy in. This can have a significant effect on your start-up costs, the amount of equipment you require and the type of establishment you want to run. If you decide to serve ready-made meals, you need to find reliable suppliers. The Caterer and Hotelkeeper Information Line* can provide a useful starting point.

- If you choose to take out a business lease or buy premises, the initial capital outlay is likely to be substantial, although costs will vary depending on your locality. To reduce expenses, you may be able to develop a venue within other premises, such as a theatre or sports complex.

- There are rules covering how prices should be displayed in restaurants and bars; for information on these contact your local trading standards department.

- If you want to run a pub, the Brewers & Licensed Retailers Association (BLRA)* publishes a free leaflet called *Thinking of Running a Pub?*

Premises

Location is a key factor when looking for retail premises. Before signing up for any premises, do your own research. Observe various locations at different times of the day, week and year, and even in diverse weather conditions.

Scan the business sections of the local paper, and keep your eyes open when driving around the district for useful leads. You can contact your local Chamber of Trade and Commerce and make yourself known to the local branch of Federation of Small Businesses* to find out when shops are likely to change hands.

Good locations include those near:

- schools, colleges, offices and industrial estates, which draw people to the area from Monday to Friday – though these people won't be around on Saturdays, the busiest shopping day of the week
- amenities, such as a swimming-pool, a central library, council offices, a museum or art gallery
- a railway station, bus terminus or taxi firm
- where people have to pause – next to a pedestrian crossing, a bus stop, or near a parking place
- other shops selling different things – but observe closely: even thriving shopping areas have their dead areas, where the trade is slower.

If you are considering shop premises that are currently empty, find out what sort of shop was there previously, how long ago and why it closed down. It might be a dead site.

The best locations may be less important for specialist shops, such as a builders' merchant or musical instrument shop, as customers may be more prepared to go a little out of the way to reach them. Such businesses may also depend less on passing trade than on becoming known and establishing a reputation.

Bad locations include those in areas with:

- a high unemployment rate
- closed-down factories
- a number of 'for sale' boards on private houses that remain for a long time
- many shops for sale or rent
- shopping centres within easy reach by car, which draw residents away.

Competing shops

You'll have to decide whether it's wise or foolish to set up near a competing business. You might, for example, be planning to run an open-all-hours general store or newsagent in a residential area.

You'll probably not want a location where there is competition a few hundred yards up the road, unless you are very sure you can attract the existing shop's customers by getting a much better site and providing a superior service.

But setting up near competition can be beneficial. People are willing to travel to clusters of competing shops selling similar things. They wander from one to the other and enjoy the choice on offer. Antique shops, gift shops, estate agents, cafes and restaurants are examples of types of business that can gain a collective benefit from being close together.

If you are looking at an area with no competition and perhaps no other shops, try to work out why no one has tried to open a business there before. If the premises have not previously been used as a shop, you may need planning permission.

Buying a going concern

If you decide to take over a shop that is at present trading, find out why the owner is selling. The reasons may be genuine – ill-health, retirement, moving on to a new business in a different area. Nevertheless, you must be sceptical.

- Has the owner been unable to make a success of the business? If so, could you? Scrutinise the accounts. Observe the owner at work. Is the owner idle or incompetent? Is the shop understocked or overstocked, understaffed or overstaffed? Are the opening hours, choice of goods, décor and general ambience poor? Or is the location simply wrong for the type of shop?

- Does the owner know about a huge new supermarket to be built nearby or of a large local factory closing down, a new main road that will cut the shopping area in two or a new one-way system? All could damage trade. The local planning authority and enquiries in the neighbourhood may be able to provide answers.

- If you think the business may be worth buying, how much will it cost to refit it if the fixtures and fittings are not to your liking? How much is the goodwill really worth? Are regular customers likely to transfer their custom to you?

Preparing the premises

When you buy premises, plan any redecoration and changes to fixtures and fittings carefully. Fittings have to last a long time and penny-pinching at the initial stage might prove a false economy later on. Visit any relevant trade exhibitions that concentrate on shop fitting, self-service and display equipment (see *Exhibition Bulletin,*★ in reference libraries).

Make a list of your requirements and a provisional sketch of the layout. You will need space to store stock and allow staff (if any) to take short breaks. Check that delivery vehicles have easy access to your premises. The shop should allow customers to move around freely and goods must be accessible. Make sure queues at the till won't create a bottleneck.

Plan a visual display that will draw in customers and encourage them to buy. The display should appear fresh, uncluttered and up to date. A shop-window should be well lit, eye-catching and changed fairly often. Products you want to promote will need pride of place. When you know exactly what you want, get estimates from several firms of specialist shop-fitters, choosing the one that will do to a good job and offer value for money.

Stock

Shops invest a large proportion of capital in stock. A good stock-control system will track sales and wastage (that is, lost, damaged and stolen goods) and guide future purchases. Keep proper records and a constant check on what goes out. You must order and re-order in plenty of time: suppliers do not always meet delivery dates and may themselves run out of some products. A computer with the appropriate software can help in stock control. It can also indicate the profitability of various types of stock. Aim for a rapid turnover of stock.

Do not be tempted to overstock by an attractive quantity discount. The ideal is to buy only what your customers want and no more than you can sell. A mixture of common sense, flair and experience should help you stock the right things. Try not to run out of anything, especially the most popular lines. Customers expect to find what they want when they want it and they go elsewhere rather than wait for it to be ordered. You may be able to offer an ordering service for products you do not normally stock, but you need to weigh up the competitive edge this may give you against the extra administration and possibly poorer margins: there are often surcharges or reduced trade discounts for small orders.

Store stock so that it does not deteriorate or acquire that grubby, shop-worn look – it's a turn-off for customers. And always rotate stock so that goods bought earliest go on sale first.

Where to buy stock

You could buy from:

- a symbol group (see below)
- a wholesaler
- a cash-and-carry warehouse (a kind of retailers' supermarket)
- directly from a manufacturer.

Look into the pros and cons of buying direct from manufacturers. If you have damaged goods, manufacturers' reps have facilities for exchange or credit, which a symbol group or cash-and-carry store may not provide. A keen rep can use these facilities to give you a little extra discount on purchases. Also, manufacturers are less likely than wholesalers to run out of stock – and lost sales lead to lost customers.

However, if you stock many items, indirect buying has the advantage that you can cut the time it takes to accept and check deliveries. Much of your stock will arrive on one van, or will be collected by you from one address in the case of a cash-and-carry. There will also be less paperwork.

Symbol groups

Some shopkeepers (especially in the grocery trade) can join a voluntary symbol group. It's a retailers' buying organisation – for example, SPAR in the grocery trade. Not only do you receive the discounts that manufacturers offer to bulk-buyers but there may also be other advantages: for example, a fascia with the group's symbol and the shop's name, help with the layout and fixtures, national promotions and advertising. Some groups offer start-up help, to find premises and provide finance. In return, you agree to take a certain amount of goods from the designated wholesaler for the area and stock a certain number of the organisation's own-brand products. You are free to buy additional goods from agencies other than the designated wholesaler.

You must offer some evidence of financial security, such as a bank reference. If you are already in business, the wholesaler will inspect your premises to see that they are in line with the organisation's requirements. If there are other shops belonging to the particular symbol group in the neighbourhood, the wholesaler may refuse to take on another.

Details of symbol groups are listed in the *Grocer Marketing Directory*★ available from the publishers (or try your reference library) and in the trade press.

Initial stocks

It's always important to have a well-stocked shop, but especially so when you first open. Customers are unlikely to come back if they find your shop wanting on their first visit. Plan your opening carefully. Choose about 20 top-selling lines and be prepared for very low profit margins on these. Select the best items from each source of supply. The initial stocking of the shop is likely to be your largest single stock buying for a long time: you may get a bulk-buy discount on this order.

This is also the time to build up a relationship with the representatives of the major firms (probably four to eight), whose products are likely to account for a large part of your turnover. They will have a good idea of competitive retail prices for particular products, and they may help with promotional allowances or by providing money-off coupons for customers. But also check other sources of supply that may be cheaper – a symbol group (see above) or a good cash-and-carry.

You may be able to negotiate extended credit from your supplier, perhaps no payment for two months, then one-sixth of your opening order to be paid for over the following six months.

Unsold stock

Some products deteriorate rapidly – for example, flowers and fresh food – while others have sell-by dates or shelf-life limits and must not be sold after a certain time. Products may go out of fashion – for example, clothes and shoes – or simply just not sell. Unsold stock takes up valuable storage space. It ties up cash and doesn't bring in money to buy new stock. It also creates a bad impression if it's on display. You should hold a seasonal sale or sell off unwanted stock at a marked-down price, week by week or day by day, depending on the goods.

Preventing burglary

You cannot make your shop totally burglar-proof but can take all precautions to minimise the risk. Before you start trading, consult:

- the crime prevention officer at your local police station
- your insurance company, which may lay down security precautions before agreeing to cover you
- a good security firm that can inspect the premises including the basement and attic, install all necessary devices, such as locks and/or bolts on all doors and windows and a burglar alarm – make sure everything complies with fire regulations.

Other simple precautions include: accounting for keys at all times; locking up every time you close and keeping a light on all night. Most insurance companies insist you leave the till open at night – a burglar would open it anyway and cause unnecessary damage. Do not have large sums of money in the shop at any time; get it banked, using the night safe after banking hours.

If you are burgled, good stock control systems will make it easier to list what has been stolen and get your claim settled more promptly.

Shoplifting

However alert you try to be, it is impossible to watch all corners of your business the whole time. Consider renting a closed-circuit TV system to monitor customer movement. Its visible presence can deter shoplifters. Place the monitor screen so that customers can also see it. Strategically placed convex mirrors can help, too, and are relatively cheap. Your shop should be well lit, with no murky corners, and shelves or racks of goods should have full light on them. You can chain expensive items to the stands and use an electronic system that alerts you if they are moved. Security firms specialising in shop protection can advise on other anti-theft devices.

Vigilance is essential, but you should never challenge suspicious customers until they have removed an article from the premises. You can then make a citizen's arrest if something has been stolen and you have good grounds for suspecting a particular person of the theft. But if the suspect is taken to court and acquitted, the arrest would be unlawful and you may have to pay damages.

Consumer protection

A shopkeeper must comply with a range of laws. Civil laws include the Sale of Goods Acts, the Supply of Goods and Services Act and the Unfair Contract Terms Act. Criminal laws include the Trade Descriptions Act, the Fair Trading Act, the Food Safety Act and the Weights and Measures Act. The Consumer Protection Act deals with certain civil and criminal matters. You can get advice from your local trading standards department.

Booklets outlining basic consumer rights are available from the Office of Fair Trading Publications,* while the booklet *A Trader's Guide: Law Relating to the Supply of Goods and Services* can also be supplied by the Department of Trade and Industry (DTI).* Croner's* reference books give invaluable explanatory notes on selected Acts of Parliament as well as other useful information and should be available in large reference libraries.

Price fixing

It is illegal for suppliers to insist that you sell goods for a minimum price, or to try to impose a minimum price by threatening to withhold supplies or discriminating in other ways. They can suggest a resale price but must not make it compulsory or take reprisals against you if you sell for less. Suppliers must not enter agreements or adopt practices that prevent, restrict or distort competition within the UK. Nor must they abuse a dominant market position by, for example, imposing unfair prices or limiting production.

If you have evidence of price fixing, contact the Office of Fair Trading.* If you think that you have been harmed as a result of a breach of the law, you may be able to claim for damages. For information, contact the Competition Act Enquiry Line.*

Sale of goods

Consumers have statutory rights or terms (known as conditions) that are triggered every time goods are sold, and thus a contract is automatically created. There are three key conditions.

- Goods must correspond with the description applied to them – whether orally, on the container, packaging, wrapping, labelling or other advertising.
- They must be of satisfactory quality – durable, safe and free from minor defects.
- They must be fit for the particular purpose. They must work properly and be well made. They must be fit for the particular purpose that the buyer wants them for, whether that is an ordinary purpose or an extraordinary or unusual one. When you tell a customer something will meet a particular requirement, it must be reasonably fit for the purpose specified. If you don't know whether or not it will meet the customer's needs, make it clear that you cannot advise the customer.

Second-hand, reduced and shop-soiled goods are also all protected by the legislation. But customers cannot claim that goods are unsatisfactory where:

- you drew the buyer's attention to the faults or defects being complained about before the sale was made, or
- the buyer examined the goods before the sale was made and should have seen the faults or defects being complained about.

Breach of any of these conditions is a breach of contract, and you as shopkeeper must put the matter right. A customer can reject the goods, reclaim the purchase price in full and claim compensation for any loss or damage resulting from the contract being broken. For example, a customer could claim the cost of re-papering and painting where a faulty cooker has exploded causing damage to the kitchen walls and ceiling. Claims are against you, but you in turn can claim against the supplier or manufacturer.

Customers must exercise their right to reject goods within a reasonable amount of time after purchase. What is reasonable depends on the facts of the case and the type of goods. Customers have the right to examine the goods properly before the right to reject them is lost. A customer, for example, could still reject a set of skis bought at the end of the skiing season and not used until the following winter, when faults were discovered. A customer loses the right to reject goods if they are not returned in a reasonable time but may still have a right to compensation, such as the cost of a repair.

You are not obliged to give a refund or exchange when customers simply change their mind about goods that have nothing wrong with them. Any refund or exchange is purely a gesture of goodwill.

Supply of goods and services

Goods supplied as part of a service (or on hire or in part exchange) must fulfil the same conditions as the sale of goods (see above). Customers can expect any service paid for to be carried out with reasonable care and skill, within a reasonable time and at a reasonable price – or at a fixed time or a fixed price if this has already been agreed between the parties. A hairdresser providing a cut and blow-dry, for example, must use the reasonable standard of care and skill that would be expected of a reasonably competent member of the hairdressing profession. Customers must authorise any work you do. They do not have to pay for work done over and above what was agreed.

Protecting customers' right

Most retailers give receipts to customers but there is no legal obligation to do so in common law. If your shop issues receipts, you cannot deny customers their rights because they do not produce the receipt. They may have lost it or you may have forgotten to give one. In law, a customer can prove a purchase with a till receipt, a credit card voucher, a cheque that has been banked and cleared or verbally – by simply stating that the goods were bought from the retailer. Signs saying such things as: 'Refunds cannot be given in the absence of a written receipt' imply to the customer that complaints will be dealt with only on written proof of purchase. They are illegal.

It is a criminal offence for a shopkeeper or a manufacturer to deny customers their statutory rights, whether by a display notice, a written contract, a wrapper, label, packaging or advertisement. The local trading standards or consumer protection department can prosecute you for the following statements: 'no money refunded'; 'for hygiene purposes, goods cannot be returned or money refunded'; 'sale goods, no money refunded' and 'credit notes only for faulty goods'. You could be fined and/or imprisoned.

Unfair contract terms

You cannot introduce unfair terms into your contract with the customer. Broadly, an unfair contract term unduly weighs the contract against the consumer and in favour of the business. A dissatisfied customer could take you to court and test any clause for reasonableness. The business might have a defence if it can show that it had acted in good faith: for example, by ensuring that the consumer fully understood the term and agreed to it freely without having been pressured to do so. Terms likely to be regarded as unfair include your right to terminate the contract without notice, a right to increase the price, penalty clauses and restrictions on a customer's statutory rights to a legal remedy.

Standard terms are those set in advance and not negotiated individually with the customer. They are typically found in the printed conditions of business on the backs of invoices or quotations. They could be challenged as unfair. Terms that are explicitly required or permitted by law and terms that define the main subject matter of the contract and the price are okay unless they are unduly difficult to understand.

You cannot avoid your liability with exclusion clauses. You might, for example, exclude liability for the loss of articles left for servicing or for the late delivery of goods promised by a certain time. A court could decide that the clause is not reasonable. Any clause excluding liability for death or personal injury caused by negligence will be void.

You can get a guidance note on unfair terms from Office of Fair Trading Publications.*

Trade descriptions

It is a criminal offence for anyone running a business to sell or offer for sale goods that are falsely described. This applies to all aspects of retailing, including advertisements, display cards, illustrations, labelling, packaging, brochures, ticketing and statements made verbally. It also covers descriptions of quality, quantity, size, method or process of manufacture, composition, performance, fitness for purpose, testing, approval by any person, previous history of the goods, place or date of manufacture or processing, and name of manufacturer.

It is a criminal offence for traders to make statements they know to be false about the provision of services, accommodation and facilities. You may commit an offence, for example, if you give an invoice stating that you have carried out certain repairs that you have not carried out.

The local trading standards or consumer protection department can prosecute you for breach of trade descriptions laws. You could be fined and/or imprisoned. They have the power to make test purchases, enter premises and inspect and seize goods and documents. You commit an offence if you wilfully obstruct a trading standards officer, deliberately fail to comply with a valid request by an officer, or do not give any other assistance asked for without reasonable cause.

If you are prosecuted for inaccurately describing a service, you can defend yourself by trying to prove that you did not know, and could not with reasonable diligence have found out, that the service did not match the description. Or you could try to prove that the description had not been applied to the service. This defence does not apply if you are supplying goods.

Whether it is goods or services that you are selling, you have a defence in cases where an offence has been committed through mistake or an accident, or through reliance on information supplied to you, or through the act or default of another person, or some other cause beyond your control. You must show that you 'took all reasonable precautions' and 'exercised all due diligence' to avoid committing an offence.

Origin marking

You must state the origin of imported goods if they are presented in a way that would give customers the impression that they were made in a particular place when they were not made there. You can get *Trade Descriptions Act – Origin Marking* from the Department of Trade and Industry (DTI).*

Displaying prices

You must show prices by writing in an unambiguous, easily identifiable, clearly legible and visible way without the customer having to ask the price. Display the price on the goods themselves or on a ticket or notice near them, or group the price with others on a list near the goods. In larger shops, you must reveal the unit price on goods sold in bulk or pre-packed in quantity. There are other rules on displaying prices.

- **VAT** You must include VAT in the displayed price if you sell mainly to private consumers. You can show VAT separately if you sell mainly to business customers.
- **Compulsory charges** You must include delivery charges and any other charges the customer *has* to pay as prominently as the basic price.
- **Charges for the payment method** You may want to charge different amounts for the same goods or services depending on the method of payment: for example, by adding a percentage for payment by credit card or a fee for payment by cheque. You must state the methods of payment to which any displayed price does not apply. You must show the difference between the displayed price and any other price as a percentage or as an amount of money. You must put notices at public entrances to the shop and at points of payment. You are also allowed to mark items individually with two or more prices.
- **Foreign currency** If you state that you accept foreign currency, you must show either the price in that foreign currency or the conversion rate (and make it clear that this does not apply to purchases by foreign-currency credit or debit card).

There are special rules relating to the prices of jewellery, precious metals, motor fuel and goods sold by mail order.

Misleading prices

It is a criminal offence for which you can be fined to give a misleading price indication on goods, services, accommodation or facilities. The rules cover price indications about:

- the actual price that the consumer will have to pay (e.g., it's an offence to indicate a price for goods that is lower than the price you are actually going to charge)
- any conditions attached to a price
- the way in which a price will be calculated
- what is expected to happen to a price in future
- price comparisons.

The local trading standards or consumer protection department enforces the rules. Consult them if you are unsure what is allowed. They have the same powers for price indications as for trade descriptions (see above).

If you are taken to court for giving a misleading price indication, the court can take into account whether or not you followed the *Code of Practice for Traders on Price Indications* produced by the Department of Trade and Industry (DTI)* – though this may not be an absolute defence. If you haven't followed the code, it may be difficult to establish that you took 'due diligence'. The code covers a number of areas, each of which is important.

Comparisons with your own previous price

These should be fair and meaningful and should always state the previous price as well as the lower price. In any comparison with the trader's own previous price:

- the previous price should be the last price at which the product was available to consumers in the previous six months
- the product should have been available to consumers at that price for at least 28 consecutive days in the previous six months
- the previous price should have applied for that period at the same shop where the reduced price is now being offered.

Where these conditions are met, the price indication is unlikely to be misleading. If you don't meet these conditions, you must give a clear explanation of the period and the circumstances in which the higher price applied (though this is not always necessary for perishables) and display it as prominently as the current price. Here are some examples.

- 'January Sale. Price £4.50. Previous price £9 from 10 to 31 December'.
- 'These goods were on sale here at the higher price from 1 February to 26 February'.
- 'These goods were on sale at the higher price in only 10 of our 95 stores'.

Comparisons with recommended retail prices and similar descriptions

All higher price descriptions should be written out in full and shown as prominently as the price, except for 'RRP' (recommended retail price) and 'man. rec. price' (manufacturer's recommended price). An RRP is a price recommended to you by the manufacturer or supplier at which the product might be sold to customers. It must not be significantly higher than prices at which the product was generally sold when you first make the comparison, and there must be a normal commercial relationship between you and the manufacturer or supplier.

Comparisons with worth or value

You must not compare your price with what something might be worth or its 'value': for example, you should not say 'worth £10, our price £5'.

Introductory offers

An introductory offer should run only for a reasonable period – generally weeks, not months. Otherwise the description becomes misleading. You must not describe prices as introductory offers unless you intend to continue to sell the item after the offer period is over and do so it at a higher price.

An offer is unlikely to be misleading if you state the date that the offer will end, and keep to it. If you extend the offer period, you must make it clear that this has been done.

Comparisons with future prices

If you quote a future 'after sale' or 'after promotion' price comparison, you should be certain that you will continue to offer identical items at that price for at least 28 days in the three months after the end of the offer period, or after the offer stocks run out. Do not use initials such as 'ASP' (after sale price) or 'APP' (after promotion price). Write the words in full as prominently as the price.

Unsafe goods

It is a criminal offence to supply consumer goods that are not reasonably safe 'having regard to all the circumstances'. You can be fined or imprisoned or both if you breach the safety laws. The circumstances could include the manner in which the goods are marketed; any warnings or instructions given with them; the means, if any, and cost of making the goods safe; and any published safety standards. If you are prosecuted, you can defend yourself by trying to prove that you neither knew, nor had reasonable grounds for believing, that the goods failed to comply with the general safety requirement.

Safety regulations detail how specific products must be constructed, and what instructions and warnings must be given. There are regulations covering the flammability of upholstered furniture, for example, as well as the safety of children's goods and toys. For information on specific products contact the Department of Trade and Industry (DTI).★

Trading standards officers can seize unsafe goods and issue suspension notices prohibiting suppliers from selling offending goods. They can apply to the courts for goods to be forfeited and destroyed.

Defective goods

Strict liability for unsafe products lies with the producer, the importer and the brand-owner of the product. In certain limited circumstances, other suppliers may be liable including the retailer. Strict liability means the accountable people are responsible regardless of whether they were at fault in any way. More information is available in *The General Product Safety Regulations 1994:*

Guidance for Businesses, Consumers and Enforcement Authorities (95/696) from DTI Consumer Safety Publications.★

Consumer credit

You can decide which customers you are prepared to offer deferred payment terms, by providing credit (see chapter 16). You don't have to give reasons for refusing a customer credit. However, customers are entitled to know the name and address of the credit reference agencies you have used (if any) so that they can check the information held.

If you want to give credit, the Consumer Credit Act and its regulations set the rules on licensing, credit references, credit cards or tokens, credit advertising, the giving of credit quotations and agreement forms for documenting credit transactions. It covers hire purchase, a conditional sale or a credit agreement for services rendered or goods supplied. It applies whether the person supplying the goods or services provides the credit facility or refers customers to a finance house. There are strict rules on advertising credit and a customer's right to a written quotation clearly stating the exact terms on which credit is on offer.

Consumer credit legislation involves many regulations and calculations. *Credit Charges* (how to calculate the total charge for credit and the annual percentage rate of charge); *Regulated and Exempt Agreements*; *Advertisements and Quotations Regulations*; *Cancellable Agreements* and *Non-cancellable Agreements*; *Hire Agreements*; and *Matters Arising During the Lifetime of an Agreement* are among publications available from the Office of Fair Trading.★

The Consumer Credit Trade Association (CCTA)★ publishes a series of short guides on the Consumer Credit Act, and provides to members both training to meet legal requirements and a personal advisory service.

Consumer credit business

Any business that provides credit under credit agreements that are regulated by the Consumer Credit Act is called a consumer credit business: for example, a shop selling goods on its own credit terms, or a finance house that supplies or finances goods under hire-purchase agreements.

Credit agreements

Before providing credit or hire facilities (such as renting out television sets or cars), you will need to ask your customer to sign an agreement that sets out the customer's rights and obligations. In many circumstances the customer has the right to cancel the agreement: if so, the agreement itself must contain a notice explaining the customer's legal rights. Various copies of the agreement must be given to the customer. There are detailed rules for the information to be given in an agreement form, and the statements of the customer's rights, which must be shown.

Licences

A person who carries on a consumer credit business must first get a credit licence. It is a criminal offence not to have one. A licence runs for five years, but it can be varied, suspended or revoked by the Office of Fair Trading* if your 'fitness' is in doubt. There are six categories of credit licence:

- category A – consumer credit business
- category B – consumer hire business
- category C – credit brokerage
- category D – debt adjusting and debt counselling
- category E – debt collecting
- category F – credit reference agency.

You must be a fit person to engage in activities covered by the licence, and the name under which you apply to be licensed must not be misleading or otherwise undesirable. To get a credit licence, and the leaflet *Do You Need a Credit Licence?*, apply to the Consumer Credit Licensing branch of the Office of Fair Trading. Licence application forms are also generally available from your local trading standards department. You can appeal if your application is turned down.

Your business is a credit brokerage if it introduces customers seeking credit to other firms offering this service. So if you sell a television and refer your customer to a company that provides credit, yet handle the paperwork yourself, you are operating a credit brokerage business. You need a Category C licence.

You need a special category of licence to canvass credit agreements for the supply of goods and services off trade premises, unless you have a written invitation to visit before credit facilities are discussed. Otherwise it is a criminal offence to canvass credit agreements for cash loans in people's homes.

Chapter 15

Becoming an exporter

Exporting can increase your market and your production, possibly bringing economies of scale that make you more competitive. Exporting can also spread the risks because you will not rely on the UK market. Different countries can go into recession at different times.

Becoming an exporter can involve:

- travelling abroad to meet your potential customers
- arranging the packing and shipment of goods
- securing payment in a world of shifting currency values and various payment methods
- complying with a variety of foreign import regulations
- setting up an export department and training staff to deal with all aspects of exporting, including increased paperwork
- added business risks (e.g. a ferry or lorry workers dispute in France, or political tensions, coups, terrorism and war almost anywhere in the world).

You could give some of these extra jobs to an export house, which may run an import/export business itself. It may act as your agent or as an agent for overseas clients to place orders with UK manufacturers. The British Exporters Association (BExA)* provides an information exchange for members.

Even if you intend to take control of your export business in the long run, you could consider using an export house initially while you concentrate on the manufacturing side of your business and developing your UK market. It is often advisable to build up your own export department gradually – for example, by employing part-time, retired export specialists and training existing staff –

while your export business becomes more solid. The Institute of Export★ provides education and training in exporting and business-information services.

Finding your customers

Research and pick your foreign markets carefully by finding out which countries are most likely to buy what you have to sell. Consider any cultural differences that may make your product especially suitable or especially inappropriate. You should also research product regulations on health, safety and so on in different countries, as your product must meet the other country's minimum standards and specifications. Plenty of advice, help and support is available, particularly from the Department of Trade and Industry (DTI).★ The A to Z listing at the DTI Trade Partners UK★ website covers the most useful sources.

- The trade press and business sections of the national press may give you ideas and information.
- Your nearest Business Link★ (or the alternatives outside England) is a good first point of contact (some have export counsellors). Also look at Invest.uk,★ Wales Trade International,★ Scottish Trade International★ and Invest Northern Ireland.★
- The DTI publishes a range of export publications giving background information on a specific market or a more detailed look at the opportunities for particular products or services within that market. Contact DTI Publications Orderline.★
- The DTI Information Centre★ has details on export markets including overseas statistical publications, foreign trade and phone directories, market surveys of overseas markets, mail-order catalogues and development plans. It can carry out research for a fee.
- DTI country desks provide information on particular countries (e.g., on import duties, local taxes and exchange controls).
- DTI Business in Europe Hotline★ supplies information on export issues within Europe, as well as a network of European Information Centres.

- DTI TradeUK★ can give possible sales leads, categorised by products, sectors and markets.
- DTI Export Explorer★ scheme allows small and inexperienced exporters to visit popular European marketplaces and trade fairs. An experienced exporter can help set up appointments with possible customers.
- British Chambers of Commerce (BCC)★ Export Marketing Research Scheme can help with research.
- Technical Help to Exporters★ (part of the British Standards Institution) gives technical information and advice on foreign regulations and standards.
- Croner's★ reference books for exporters provide information on all aspects of the export trade, with separate entries for every country, giving a summary of its individual import regulations. These should be available in a reasonably large reference library.
- You could join a trade fair or mission to explore overseas markets. The DTI supports some financially. The British Chambers of Commerce produces a trade mission handbook.
- Commercial attachés at the British embassies and foreign embassies in London may be able to help.
- The National Languages for Export Campaign offers various services to exporters. Consult your local Business Link (or the alternatives outside England). You may need promotional material in a foreign language, translators and interpreters.
- The International Chamber of Commerce★ can advise on contracts with overseas agents, which should be watertight.
- The Simpler Trade Procedures Board (SITPRO)★ has a helpdesk for procedural, payment and documentation queries.

Agreeing a price

In order to calculate the price to your customer abroad, you must take into account:

- discounts for cash or quantity
- any extra costs for export packaging
- cost of freight and transportation
- bank charges imposed by the bank through which you receive payment – they depend on the payment method chosen

- any costs for currency exchange
- cost of insurance for the goods in transit (when your responsibility for the goods ceases depends on the terms agreed with your customer) and possibly for credit insurance
- commission for your agent abroad, if you have one.

Sending the customer a quote

All terms should be clearly set out in a quotation, in the form of a pro-forma invoice to the customer. It becomes a binding contract on both parties once the customer has accepted it. The customer may confirm the order by fax or email and should also send a letter of confirmation.

A pro-forma invoice looks like an ordinary invoice, except for the words 'pro-forma' in the heading. It should indicate the:

- type and quantity of goods
- price details
- delivery time
- terms of payment (such as letter)
- currency in which the deal is to be made
- method of packing
- how long your offer remains valid.

The pro-forma invoice should also show which International Chamber of Commerce (ICC)* Incoterms (standard trade terms) apply and are included in the quotation by way of transport and insurance, for example:

- free alongside ship (f.a.s.) – the price includes freight charges to the docks (named port)
- free on board at named port (f.o.b.) – the price includes freight charges on to the ship
- carriage paid to … (CPT) – the price includes freight charges to a named port of destination
- carriage and insurance paid to …(CIP) – the price includes both freight and insurance charges to an agreed port of destination.

Full details of the Incoterms are available from the ICC.

Dealing with suppliers

If your business is exporting someone else's goods, you will need to contact the manufacturer or stockist for quotations (unless you have the goods in stock). You must emphasise that the goods will have to be suitably packaged for export.

The supplier's quotation or pro-forma invoices should be with prices quoted f.o.b. or CIP (see above), as requested. If a supplier will quote only f.o.b., you must estimate the cost of freight, insurance if required and shipping expenses. Ask the supplier for an approximate shipping specification: the number of packages, cartons, cases, etc. that will be needed, the delivery time, their gross and net weights and their shipping measurements.

Make sure all the details on the supplier's quotation match those on the pro-forma invoice that you give the customer. The supplier's descriptions and the customer's requirements must be the same, as, once the order is placed, a customer will usually insist on receiving goods exactly as specified.

Delivering your goods

For sending goods by sea or air you will normally need the services of a freight forwarder, who should be a registered trading member of the British International Freight Association (BIFA).* BIFA can supply names of their members as well as *A Brief Introduction to Freight Transport*. A freight forwarder can:

- advise on the best method of transportation to the destination, depending on your requirements for speed, safety and cost
- prepare most of the shipping and customs documents
- arrange marine insurance, if required
- attend to other shipping details
- get bills of lading or sea waybills.

Shipping companies issue bills of lading, detailed receipts for the goods and a document of title to the goods listed on it. A bill contains a contract whereby the shipper undertakes to deliver the goods to a specified port of destination. A bill of lading is now increasingly superseded by the non-negotiable sea waybill, which is not a document of title but enables the consignee (shipper) to clear the goods without acquiring a title to them.

If they are going by deep-sea liner, goods are usually moved in containers. They may be packed inland before being taken to the docks. Each may hold several different consignments. Goods to short-sea destinations in Ireland and Europe are usually moved on road vehicles straight on to the ferries. This allows a more rapid distribution of goods.

Forwarding freight by air is fairly similar to forwarding freight by sea. The goods are generally collected by the air freight forwarder and taken into its premises prior to being delivered to the airline sheds at the airport. Many forwarders will give quotations on a door-to-door basis. The document of carriage is called an air waybill, and is not a document of title. Express air services can send goods rapidly. These overnight carriers deal directly with exporters, use simple documentation and arrange for goods to be cleared through customs.

Exporting by post

You can send goods directly to your customers by post if they are neither bulky nor heavy. The procedure is simple: you complete the appropriate customs declaration forms (obtainable from the post office) and either attach them to the parcel or hand them in when posting. Goods sent by post, courier or fast-parcel services within the European Union (EU) do not need customs declarations, providing you use a special despatch pack (check with the post office).

Every country has its own regulations on customs declaration forms, packing and prohibited goods. Consult the post office when despatching each consignment. More details are available from a Royal Mail Sales Centre.★

Customs

Very few forms are now required if you are exporting within the EU. Outside the EU, however, you will need to contact your local Customs and Excise enquiry centre for the relevant documentation. As the exporter, you are responsible for completing the customs declaration correctly, even if someone else fills in the forms, for example, the freight forwarder acting as the agent.

VAT on exports

Exports to a country outside the EU are zero-rated for VAT (see Chapter 8), provided strict conditions are met. So are exports to businesses within the EU.

- You must despatch the goods to a destination outside the UK and have evidence that this has happened.
- If you are exporting within the EU, you must show the customer's VAT-registration number with a prefix showing the country (your own VAT number must be prefixed 'GB').
- You must send Customs and Excise a regular list of exports to VAT-registered EU customers.
- You must meet extra conditions to qualify for zero-rating, if you have a EU business customer who is not VAT-registered.
- If you are selling to private individuals in the EU, you are technically 'distance selling' and must normally charge UK VAT. If your sales to one EU country exceed that country's annual VAT threshold, you will have to register for VAT in that country.
- Exports to a UK export house do not qualify for zero-rating.

For more details, get *Exports and Removals of Goods from the UK*, *VAT Retail Exports*, *Should I Be Registered for VAT?*, *Distance Selling* and *The Single Market* from Customs & Excise.★

Methods of payment

The four most common methods of payment for export orders are: cash with order or before delivery; documentary letter of credit; payment against documentary collection and direct payment. They are listed below in descending order of security.

Cash with order or before delivery

Cash payment at the same time as the order or before it is delivered is the ideal way to be paid, though you may not get it. In any case, such transactions may be prohibited under local exchange-control regulations.

Documentary letter of credit

With a documentary letter of credit, your customer opens a letter of credit in your favour. The customer's bank instructs a bank in the UK to pay you the agreed amount on production of a correct and complete set of documents and on satisfying any other agreed conditions.

There are different types of letters of credit. The safest but hardest to get is an irrevocable letter of credit confirmed (underwritten) by a recognised bank in Britain. Payment is guaranteed in all circumstances – revolution, currency crash, insolvency and Act of God.

Other forms of letters of credit include unconfirmed irrevocable credits and revocable letters of credit. They are not secure because payment can be stopped. Use them if the country's exchange controls require a letter of credit and the customer is trustworthy. *UCP 500* from the International Chamber of Commerce (ICC)★ gives details of what is regarded as a letter of credit.

The documents required for letters of credit will be listed in the bank's advice of the credit, and may include one or possibly several copies of the following:

- the original letter of credit
- the exporter's commercial invoice, signed (not the pro-forma, although it contains the same information)
- the bill of lading or a receipted waybill
- the insurance policy or certificate
- bill of exchange or a sight draft (which are demands for payment)
- a certificate of origin (issued and certified by a designated UK Chamber of Commerce) specifying the origin of the goods – you can get details of designated Chambers in the UK from the British Chambers of Commerce (BCC)★
- export and import licences
- inspection certificates
- health certificates
- consular invoices.

Whether or not all these documents are specified in the letter of credit, many will be required by the customer for import purposes.

All documents must conform in every particular to the requirements of the letter of credit and to the customer's order: the type and quantity of the goods, the marks (which identify the goods) and the measurements of the packing cases. The bank is likely to withhold payment if there are any discrepancies. The customer will be unable to claim the goods until the documents arrive (forwarded by the bank) and will want reimbursement from you for the warehouse storage costs if they are late. Take advice from someone experienced in the export trade to avoid problems.

Payment against documentary collection

Payment against documentary collection should be used only with a tried-and-proven customer. Banks act as intermediaries but offer no guarantee of payment. The customer undertakes to pay when the documents that prove ownership arrive at the bank overseas or the goods arrive at the destination. The customer can claim the goods when the bank hands over the documents after payment is made. The same documents as for a letter of credit are required (see above).

You must specify the terms of payment. You can ask for payment either on sight of the documents or 30, 60 or 90 days after the customer receives them. Include a reasonable allowance for interest in the price and check the credit rating of the customer if you are prepared to give extended payment terms.

Direct payments

You can simply send the goods and trust your customer to send you the money. Check the credit rating of your customer before quoting payment terms that do not guarantee payment, and use debt collectors if you are not paid in a reasonable time.

SWIFT is the abbreviated title of the inter-bank worldwide system for handling international electronic payments, for which there are a number of payment methods:

- international money transfer (or mail transfers) – your customer's bank instructs a correspondent bank in the UK to pay you
- express transfers – a speedier and more expensive version of international money transfers

- bankers' drafts – effectively cash in your hands, so not very secure.

When deciding which is the most suitable method of payment, take account of cost, security, speed and currency risk. You could open a local bank account to receive payments in a country where you do a lot of business.

Short-term export finance is available from several sources to help exporters with payment delays and foreign exchange fluctuations. Most major banks have export finance schemes.

Protecting against export risks

The Exports Credits Guarantee Department (ECGD)★ is the UK's official export credit insurer and the government department designed to protect exporters against some of the hazards of trading overseas. ECGD cover, if available, can be tailored to meet the particular needs of customers, who now tend to be concentrated in the capital goods and project sectors. Protection is given not only for the export of goods but also for a range of services and earnings from overseas investments.

ECGD can give an unconditional guarantee of repayment to banks that provide overseas buyers with finance to purchase UK goods. Or it can insure exporters directly against the main commercial and political risks of non-payment that can arise during the manufacturing and delivery stages of a contract. ECGD's policies allow exporters to be paid as goods are delivered or when work is completed. They also enable UK companies to extend credit terms to their overseas buyers.

Alternatively, private credit insurance has fewer restrictions on cover and the advantage of combining export and domestic cover under the terms of one policy. Insurance for goods sold on short-credit terms is now available only from the private sector. There are several private insurers, including Gerling NCM★ and Euler Trade Indemnity plc.★

Chapter 16

Getting paid

Immediate payment from customers is the ideal way to get paid, but it is often not possible, because it is not normal practice in your line of business or because you are supplying business rather than retail customers. You then risk late or non-payment and should look for ways to reduce the risk.

Ensure that your terms of business are known when the order is accepted, and invoice promptly. Your invoices should clearly show the goods or services for which you are charging, the order reference number, payment method, payment period and expected payment date. Set up a system for routinely chasing outstanding payments. *Better Payment Practice: A Guide to Credit Management* is available free from the DTI Publications Orderline.★

You should also aim to pay your bills on time. Payment problems can have a domino effect. A supplier you don't pay on time could refuse to supply you, which in turn could make it difficult to meet customer demand. Relationships could be soured. Customers who don't pay you could cause cash-flow problems so that you struggle to find the money to pay suppliers. At worst, a major customer with problems could drive you into insolvency (see Chapter 17).

Discounts for prompt payment

Discounts for early settlement can encourage prompt payment but you need to weigh up the advantage of fast payment (and possible reductions in your overdraft costs) against the loss of profit. And when customers take the discount but still pay late, it can be difficult to recover the money. An alternative is to make future discounts conditional on prompt payment.

Interest on late payment

You have a legal right to claim interest on debts paid late. The rate of interest is set at base rate plus 8 per cent at the time of writing, but this may change. You can get detailed guidance at www.payontime.co.uk. If you have specifically agreed a credit period, you can charge interest after this period ends until payment is received. If there is no agreed credit period, the payment is legally due from the moment the goods are delivered or the service performed. However, your right to charge interest starts 30 days after the invoice date or after the goods or services are delivered – whichever is later.

You may be reluctant to claim interest if it will jeopardise your relationship with a major customer. But if you do claim interest, inform the customer – ideally in writing – that you intend to claim, stating how much you are owed, the reason why the money is owed and how it should be paid.

Businesses that are larger than your own may force you to agree to less stringent late-payment arrangements. If so, any such agreement must be fair, reasonable and enough to have either a deterrent or a compensatory effect. Otherwise, you can apply to the courts to set it aside. *The Late Payment of Commercial Debts (Interest) Act 1998: A User's Guide* is available from the DTI Publications Orderline.*

Assessing customers' credit-worthiness

There are various ways of evaluating your customer's creditworthiness before you let them have high-value goods or services.

- The grapevine can help. Contact other businesses in the area, as they may have had problems getting paid or know of impending problems with a particular customer.
- Ask the customer for a bank reference. The bank will charge for this, and will need permission from the customer. Ask specific questions such as 'Do you consider XYZ good for £5,000 on 30-day terms?' The reference will speak in what is effectively a coded language: for this reason, you should not place sole reliance on them.

- Credit agencies provide details of potential customers, their financial results, the payment experience of other suppliers, county court judgements, outstanding loans and a credit rating. You can either take out a subscription to a database, or buy reports on a one-off basis. You may be able to get a report through your local Business Link* (or the alternatives outside England). Many have their own subscriptions.
- Publicly quoted companies now have an obligation to give details of their payment performance in their annual report and accounts. The Federation of Small Businesses has developed league tables in collaboration with Dun & Bradstreet Europe Ltd,* the business information company.

Accepting plastic cards

You may decide to try to make payment terms easier for your customers, and possibly attract more business, by becoming a merchant of one or both of the principal international card payment systems: Mastercard and Visa. You could also consider American Express and Diners Club. Plastic credit cards are not appropriate for some businesses, such as small food shops and others where the amount of a transaction and/or profit margin is low, as the extra costs involved may make them uneconomic. But for many businesses they are essential, and the additional expenses are worth paying for the increased sales such cards generate. Indeed, in some types of business, you risk losing significant sales if you do not accept plastic credit and debit cards.

You pay around 4 to 5 per cent (for small businesses) for each credit card transaction, and a flat-rate handling fee for each debit card transaction. In addition, you may want to buy or lease an electronic terminal. You can partially balance the costs of using plastic against the possible savings in costs from handling, securing and banking less cash and fewer cheques.

When a customer presents a card, you must check that:

- it has not passed its expiry date
- it has not been notified to you as lost or stolen
- the signature of the customer on the sales voucher agrees with the signature on the card.

The card company gives you a 'floor limit' if you use a manual imprinter to record details of the card. You have to get authorisation from the card company for transactions above the floor limit. You may be given an envelope in which to send your vouchers to the card company; or you may hand them over to a cashier at a bank as you would cash or cheques. If you use an electronic terminal, details of the card are recorded when you swipe it through the machine; you don't need authorisation for transactions above the floor limit and do not have to deliver vouchers to the bank.

You will receive a monthly statement from the card company summarising the transactions submitted and showing the service charge due. It will be deducted from your bank account by direct debit.

Accepting euros

You may want or have to accept euros if you have a major customer who operates internationally and decides to work in euros – or if you have a business in a tourist area. Alternatively, you may have a supplier who wants to deal in euros. You will need to take appropriate steps to accommodate the euro.

- Find out what euro services your bank offers. If much of your trade is likely to be in euros, you might consider opening a euro bank account.
- Familiarise yourself with euro symbols and banknotes, and build them into your book-keeping system and other paperwork. Find out how to print out the euro sign on your computer – fonts that include the symbol are available.
- Get tills that can deal with euros.
- Consider displaying prices in both pounds and euros. You may want to choose prices that are easy to convert – £2.99, for example, is unlikely to convert tidily.
- Decide how you would handle a request to pay in euros. Consider what conversion rate you would use. Train your staff to deal with the euro.
- If you decide to pass on the costs of converting one-off transactions to your customers, make sure they know in advance – being suspected of profiteering will definitely sour your relationship.

- If you are offered a cheque denominated in euros, check the address of the issuing bank on the cheque. If you accept cheques in euros not drawn on UK issuers, you will have to wait longer for the cheque to clear and will incur extra bank charges. These difficulties should not arise with UK-issued cheques, but there is currently no cheque guarantee scheme for them.
- If you want to work completely in euros, you can pay your UK taxes including VAT in euros, although returns and declarations will still have to be made in sterling. VAT invoices must show the sterling equivalent as well as the euro price.

The Euro and Your Business is available from the Euro Preparations Unit★ and *You and Euro Payments* from the British Bankers' Association.★ Your local Business Link★ (or the alternatives outside England) or Chamber of Commerce may also be able to help. The EuroPlanner, a disk that includes spreadsheets to set euro prices and explains how various options will affect profits, is available from the Department of Trade and Industry (DTI).★

Dealing with bad payers

Factoring

If you are in real cash-flow trouble, perhaps because you have reached your bank borrowing limit and have a lot of customers owing you money, you could think about factoring. A factoring company advances you the money owing on your customers' invoices (usually up to 80 per cent), and retains a percentage as commission when they are paid. There is usually an administration charge or service fee, which depends on volume. Firms with lots of low-value invoices may find that this fee makes factoring uneconomic.

Factoring traditionally used to be a last desperate attempt to raise money but is now becoming a much more acceptable and commercially viable way of raising finance. It is expensive but can help relieve some of the administrative burden of chasing invoices and ensures that slow-paying customers do not lock up your working capital. Consult your Business Link★ (or the alternatives outside England) or your accountant for the name of a suitable company.

Most factoring companies are backed by clearing banks or other major financial organisations. *A Guide to Factoring and Discounting* is available from the DTI Publications Orderline.★

Recovering lost money

If customers owe you money, you can apply to the county court, which can also supply a booklet on how to do this. You can buy credit insurance to guard against bad debts. The British Insurance and Investment Brokers Association (BIIBA)★ can give details of specialist brokers.

Avoiding fraud

Forged notes, bouncing cheques and stolen cards all eat into your profits, and it is a good idea to monitor your losses and take action if you see any trends emerging.

Cash fraud

Most retail businesses have to deal with transactions in old-fashioned notes and coins, so you should take steps to identify counterfeit bank notes. Ultra-violet lamps can detect forged notes, though they are not foolproof. Forgeries are supposed to become fluorescent under them, but genuine notes may also do so if they have been in contact with certain detergents.

A more reliable guide is to compare a suspect note with another that you know is genuine. A genuine note should feel crisp, not limp, waxy or shiny. The watermark should be hardly apparent until the note is held to the light. Genuine Bank of England and Scottish notes have a thread embedded in them, which should appear as a bold continuous line when held up to the light.

The Bank of England★ produces various leaflets explaining the security features of its bank notes. The Committee of Scottish Clearing Bankers★ and Northern Ireland Bankers' Association★ also produce security guidance.

Cheque fraud

Cheques can 'bounce' – be rejected by the bank – unless you insist that the customer produces a cheque card and you write its number on the back of the cheque. This guarantees payment if you took the cheque in good faith. You can insist on the customer's bank paying up to the limit set on the card, even if the chequebook and card turn out to have been stolen or the customer's account is empty.

Taking more than one guaranteed cheque for a single purchase costing over the limit invalidates the guarantee. Possibly none of the part-payment cheques would be honoured. Do not accept a cheque for more than the limit stated on the card without checking with the customer's bank or holding up delivery of the goods until the cheque has cleared.

Plastic card fraud

Shopping by mail or phone with someone else's card details is ideal for the fraudster but not for the trader. You may inadvertently make a sale to a thief and find the genuine cardholder disputes the transaction. The card issuer can charge back the transaction to your account even if you obtained authorisation, because the cardholder disputes the transaction.

To reduce the risks (you cannot eliminate them), send the goods only to the cardholder's address: do not let a third party such as a courier collect them. If the cardholder collects the goods, you should ask to see the card and obtain a signature. For large-value transactions, you could offer to ring back customers after checking details using, for example, a phone book. To confirm that the goods have been received, you could insist on some proof of receipt.

Credit and debit card companies may send you details of stolen cards from time to time, with instructions not to accept those cards. If you use a manual imprinter, it may be difficult to check every single card that is offered. Electronic terminals, however, should check cards automatically – but you cannot rely on them completely because of delays in updating the computer's records.

Card companies may refuse to accept transactions on cards that have been listed as stolen, but, if you accept a stolen credit or debit card in good faith, the issuing organisation will pay you the money. They also pay rewards for lost or stolen cards that are picked up by shops.

Liasing with other businesses

To combat fraud, consider joint action with other local businesses. You could, for example, set up some sort of 'early warning' system whereby you all agree to alert each other if someone you suspect of passing forged notes is sighted. The local crime prevention or crime reduction officer may be able to give advice on this. You should certainly ensure that your employees are trained to follow the correct procedures – without putting themselves at risk – if they do encounter a suspect customer.

Chapter 17

Fighting insolvency

Some perfectly healthy small businesses become insolvent because a major customer gets into financial difficulties and can't pay their bills. Other firms become insolvent because of their own financial difficulties. Whatever the reason, insolvency will almost certainly involve the closure of your business, but you may be able to save it.

Insolvency procedures depend on how the business is set up: sole traders file for bankruptcy while companies and partnerships are compulsorily liquidated. The Insolvency Service★ is a government agency that administers the affairs of bankrupts and companies in compulsory liquidation. You can get *A Guide to Bankruptcy* and *A Guide for Creditors* from Insolvency Service Publications.★

Some of the details in this chapter do not apply in Scotland, though many of the principles and procedures are similar.

If you are owed money

You may be a creditor – someone owed money – who wants to start insolvency proceedings. Before you take this step, assess the likely outcome as well as the fees you will have to pay to the court and official receiver and possibly your own solicitor. Take account of the likely assets of the individual or business, whether there are likely to be other creditors and where you are in the pecking order of creditors. You will have to guesstimate how much money, if any, you are likely to get back.

If another creditor has started insolvency proceedings, the official receiver or insolvency practitioner should automatically contact you if you too are a known creditor. Contact the official receiver's office nearest to the insolvent business (addresses available from the Insolvency Service) if you don't hear from them.

Avoiding compulsory insolvency

Prompt action may save you from closing your business if you experience a cash crisis, so get advice from an authorised insolvency practitioner. They are usually solicitors or accountants listed in *Yellow Pages* under 'Insolvency Practitioners' and may offer a free initial consultation. Some organisations also offer insolvency advice – despite not being suitably qualified in some instances. Be wary of cold calls and unsolicited letters offering advice. If in doubt, contact your local Business Link★ or the alternatives outside England. There is a useful website at www.insolvency.co.uk.

An insolvency practitioner may suggest you write to all your creditors asking them to accept payments according to a schedule agreed with them all. This has the advantage of cheapness but will work only if all your creditors co-operate. It still leaves you liable to bankruptcy or compulsory liquidation proceedings if any creditors change their minds.

Alternatively, an insolvency practitioner may recommend a legally binding voluntary arrangement with creditors or administration or voluntary bankruptcy/liquidation.

Voluntary arrangement with creditors

Sole traders, partnerships and companies can make legally binding voluntary arrangements with their creditors. You can apply to the court for an interim order, naming your chosen insolvency practitioner who will help you prepare the proposal for a voluntary arrangement. An interim order will stop any other legal proceedings against you or your property without the leave of the court.

Once the interim order is in force, your insolvency practitioner will enquire into your debts and report to the court on your proposal for a voluntary arrangement. The court will extend the interim order if it is satisfied with the proposal. You must then call a meeting of your creditors. If the proposal is approved by more than 75 per cent in value of the creditors present and voting at the meeting, either in person or by proxy, it will be binding on all creditors who were notified. It will then be supervised by your insolvency practitioner or another chosen by the creditors. Provided you stick to the arrangement, you will avoid bankruptcy or compulsory liquidation, and the restrictions and bad publicity that go with it.

If your creditors do not approve the proposal, the interim order will lapse and any creditors can take steps to enforce the debt.

Administration for sole traders

If your debts are less than £5,000 and there is a county court judgement for at least one of the debts, you can apply to that court for an administration order. Such an order will provide for all your debts (whether or not there are court orders relating to them) to be paid by single weekly or monthly payments to the court. If you have no prospect of paying off all your debts within a reasonable time, you can apply to the court for an order that you pay only a limited percentage of your debts. The court will accumulate the payments and distribute them to your creditors pro rata. Your creditors cannot enforce the debts by other means while you maintain the payments.

Administration for companies and partnerships

The business or its creditors can apply to the court for an administration order if there is a chance that the company can be saved as a going concern, or be sold for more than would be raised by liquidation. If the court is satisfied that the business cannot pay its debts (or is likely to become unable to), an insolvency practitioner is appointed as administrator to effect a rescue plan or sell the business. The business is given a breathing space: while it is in administration, creditors cannot take legal action to wind up the company or appoint a receiver. Administration will usually last up to 12 months but in a few cases may take longer. The business can move from administration to a voluntary arrangement with creditors (see above) or voluntary liquidation (see below).

Alternatively, secured creditors can appoint an administrator without applying to the court (they simply file a notice of appointment at court), but the administrator will have a duty to act in the interests of all creditors.

Administration is not the same as being placed in administrative receivership. This type of receivership applies only to companies and the court is not usually involved. Instead, certain major creditors (usually a bank) can appoint an insolvency practitioner as receiver to recover their money.

Voluntary bankruptcy

As a sole trader, you can present your own petition in bankruptcy on payment of a £250 deposit and a fee to the court. You must provide a statement of your affairs, with details of all your debts and assets on a form provided by the court. Where your unsecured debts are less than £20,000 the court may issue a certificate of summary administration. The advantages are that you are discharged from bankruptcy in two rather than three years, sanctions for failure to keep proper records do not apply, and the official receiver may decide not to enquire fully into your affairs.

Voluntary liquidation

A company or partnership can choose voluntary liquidation for a business that is insolvent. Voluntary liquidation can be less expensive than compulsory liquidation and leaves more money for the creditors. A solvent business can also elect for voluntary liquidation if it is sold off or decides to cease trading. An insolvency practitioner acts as the liquidator and the courts are not usually involved.

Compulsory bankruptcy

A creditor to whom you owe at least £750 as an unsecured debt can serve on you a formal demand requiring you to pay the debt or give security for it or propose an arrangement to pay off the debt under an agreed scheme of payments. If the debt is a future debt, the demand will require you to establish to the reasonable satisfaction of the creditor that you will be able to pay the debt when it falls due.

After 21 days (earlier in exceptional cases), the creditor can file a petition for bankruptcy in a bankruptcy court (the High Court in London or certain specified county courts) if you do not comply with the formal demand. The bankruptcy petition must normally be served on you personally, but the court can give permission for a substituted service – for example, the post – to be used.

The court will probably make a bankruptcy order unless you can satisfy it that:

- you have paid off the debt

- the debt is not due
- the creditor owes you an amount equal to or exceeding your debt due to the creditor
- the creditor has unreasonably refused your proposal to pay off or secure the debt
- there is a reasonable prospect that you will be able to pay the debt when it falls due, if it is a future debt.

The court can postpone a decision to enable you to make proposals to pay off or secure the debt. Securing a debt means giving the creditor a legal charge on something you own: for example, a mortgage on your home to fund your business is a secured debt. The creditor can force you to sell it if you default.

The effect of bankruptcy

As a bankrupt, all your assets (with limited exceptions) are vested in a trustee in bankruptcy. The official receiver (part of the Insolvency Service★) will act as trustee unless an insolvency practitioner is appointed. You must complete a statement of affairs giving full details of your debts and assets. If you fail to disclose your assets fully or otherwise fail to co-operate with the trustee, you may be committing an offence. You may be required to attend a public examination, at which you will be questioned about the reasons for your insolvency and how you handled your assets.

The trustee can apply to the court for an order requiring you to make regular payments out of your income towards payment of your debts. The trustee can also apply for possession of your home (if it is owned solely by you) or possession and sale (if it is owned jointly). The court must take into account the legal rights of your spouse and children to live in the home. But after one year from the date of the trustee's appointment, the court assumes (save in exceptional circumstances) that the rights of the creditors outweigh all other considerations.

It is a criminal offence:

- not to have kept proper accounting records of your business
- if, during the same business period, you materially contributed to or increased the extent of your insolvency by gambling or rash and hazardous speculation

- for you (either alone or jointly) to get credit for more than £250 without disclosing the bankruptcy
- to engage in business under a name other than that in which you were made bankrupt, without disclosing to the people with whom you trade the name in which you were made bankrupt
- for a bankrupt (except with the court's permission) either to act as a director or to be concerned in the promotion, formation or management of a limited company.

Unless you have been bankrupt previously or the court orders otherwise, you are normally discharged from bankruptcy after three years. Discharge releases you from most of your bankruptcy debts, but you remain liable for certain debts: for example, court orders requiring you to pay maintenance. And your assets in the bankruptcy remain vested in your trustee until all your debts are paid in full and the bankruptcy order is annulled. The trustee can sell them to pay off your debts.

New rules in 2004

From a date in 2004 still to be set at the time of writing, fewer restrictions will automatically be imposed on undischarged bankrupts and nearly all will be discharged after 12 months, some sooner. However, new bankruptcy restriction orders will impose more restrictions on bankrupts whose conduct before and during the bankruptcy was found wanting. They will last for between two and 15 years.

Compulsory liquidation

A company is insolvent if it cannot pay its debts or its assets amount to less than its liabilities. It can then be taken to court by a creditor, who presents a petition stating that the company owes a sum of money and that it cannot pay. The court may then issue a winding-up order, which can be cancelled or reviewed provided you apply to the court within seven days.

The effect of compulsory liquidation

When the court makes a winding-up order to liquidate the company, it puts the matter in the hands of the official receiver, who will notify creditors and others with an interest. An insolvency practitioner may be appointed to act as liquidator if there are significant assets.

- The official receiver will usually visit your premises. Trading is likely to cease. Employees (including you, if you are one) will be dismissed. You will have no control of the company's business, assets and property, but your duties and responsibilities as a director will continue: for example, you may have to help dispose of assets.
- The liquidator will sell the company's assets, pay the fees and charges arising from the liquidation, and share out any remaining funds to creditors and (very occasionally) shareholders. When the winding-up is complete, the company will be dissolved.
- As a director of the company, you will be interviewed by the official receiver at some stage. You must provide a statement of your affairs. You may be required to contribute to the company's assets if you misapplied company funds or if the company traded fraudulently or wrongfully. Wrongful trading means that you failed to minimise the potential loss to the company's creditors – even though you knew, or ought to have concluded, that the company had no reasonable prospect of avoiding insolvency.
- You may be asked to make a payment for any shares that have not been fully paid up if you are a shareholder.
- The creditor may ask you to pay off any company debts that you have guaranteed. You may be forced into bankruptcy if you cannot pay them.
- The liquidator or official receiver will send the Department of Trade and Industry (DTI)★ a report about all directors who were in office in the last three years of the company's trading. You may be considered to be guilty of misconduct or unfit to be a director: for example, because you traded wrongfully, failed to keep proper records or failed to co-operate in the

liquidation. If so, you can be disqualified from being a director for between 2 and 15 years.

Unless you are disqualified or made bankrupt, you can still act as the director of another company. However, for five years after the winding up you cannot be involved in another business with a name so similar that it suggests an association with the failed company.

Addresses and contacts

ACAS Reader Ltd
PO Box 235
Hayes
Middlesex UB3 1HF
Tel: (0870) 242 9090
Fax: 020-8867 3225
Website: www.acas.gov.uk

Advertising Standards Authority (ASA)
2 Torrington Place
London
WC1E 7HW
Tel: 020-7580 5555
Fax: 020-7631 3051
Email: inquiries@asa.org.uk
Website: www.asa.org.uk

Advisory, Conciliation and Arbitration Service (ACAS)
Brandon House
180 Borough High Street
London SE1 1LW
Tel: 020-7210 3000
Fax: 020-7210 3645
Website: www.acas.org.uk

Association of British Insurers (ABI)
51 Gresham Street
London
EC2V 7HQ
Tel: 020-7600 3333
Fax: 020-7696 8996
Email: info@abi.org.uk
Website: www.abi.org.uk

Association of Consulting Actuaries (ACA)
1 Wardrobe Place
London EC4V 5AG
Tel: 020-7248 3163
Fax: 020-7236 1889
Email: acahelp@aca.org.uk
Website: www.aca.org.uk

Bank of England
Issue Office
Threadneedle Street
London EC2R 8AH
Tel: 020-7601 4878
Fax: 020-7601 5460
Email: enquiries@bankofengland.co.uk
Website: www.bankofengland.co.uk

Booksellers Association of Great Britain and Ireland
Minster House
272 Vauxhall Bridge Road
London SW1V 1BA
Tel: 020-7802 0802
Fax: 020-7802 0803
Email: mail@booksellers.org.uk
Website: www.booksellers.org.uk

Brewers & Licensed Retailers Association (BLRA)
(See British Beer & Pub Association)

British Bankers' Association
Pinners Hall
105–108 Old Broad Street
London EC2N 1EX
Tel: 020-7216 8800
Fax: 020-7216 8811
Website: www.bba.org.uk

British Beer & Pub Association
(formerly BLRA)
Market Towers
1 Nine Elms Lane
London SW8 5NQ
Tel: 020-7627 9191
Fax: 020-7627 9123
Email:
enquiries@beerandpub.com
Website: www.beerandpub.com

British Chambers of Commerce
(BCC)
5th Floor
50 Broadway
St James' Park
London SW1H 0RG
Tel: 020-7152 4046
Fax: 020-7152 4145
Email:
info@britishchambers.org.uk
Website:
www.britishchambers.org.uk

British Exporters Association
(BExA)
Broadway House
Tothill Street
London SW1H 9NQ
Tel: 020-7222 5419
Fax: 020-7799 2468
Email: bexamail@aol.com
Website: www.bexa.co.uk

British Franchise Association
(BFA)
Thames View
Newtown Road
Henley-on-Thames
RG9 1HG
Tel: (01491) 578050
Fax: (01491) 573517
Email: mailroom@british-
franchise.org.uk
Website: www.british-
franchise.org.uk

British Institute of Innkeeping
Park House
80 Park Street
Camberley
Surrey GU15 3PT
Tel: (01276) 684449
Fax: (01276) 23045
Website: www.bii.org

British Insurance and Investment
Brokers' Association (BIBA)
BIBA House
14 Bevis Marks
London EC3A 7NT
Tel: 020-7623 9043
Fax: 020-7626 9676
Email: enquiries@biba.org.uk
Website: www.biba.org.uk

British International Freight
Association (BIFA)
Redfern House
Browells Lane
Feltham TW13 7EP
Tel: 020-8844 2266
Fax: 020-8890 5546
Email: bifa@bifa.org
Website: www.bifa.org

British Library Science Reference and Information Service
Science 1 Reading Room
Bristol Library
96 Euston Road
London NW1 2DB
Tel: 020-7412 7454/7977
Research enquiries: 020-7412 7457
Fax: 020-7412 7453
Email: patents-information@bl.uk
Website: www.bl.uk

British Telecom (BT) Telemarketing guide
Tel: (0808) 100 1293

British Venture Capital Association (BVCA)
3 Clements Inn
London WC2R 3AA
Tel: 020-7025 2950
Fax: 020-7025 2951
Email: bvca@bvca.co.uk
Website: www.bvca.co.uk

Business Connect (Wales)
Tel: (0845) 796 9798
Email:
executive@businessconnect.org.uk
Website:
www.businessconnect.org.uk

Business Link (England)
Tel: (0845) 600 9006
Website: www.businesslink.org

Capita Learning & Development
17 Rochester Row
London SW1P 1LA
Tel: (0870) 400 1000
Fax: (0870) 400 1099
Email: info@capita-ld.co.uk
Website: www.capita-ld.co.uk

Caterer and Hotelkeeper Information Line
Quadrant House
The Quadrant
Sutton
Surrey SM2 5AS
Tel: 020-8652 3423
Fax: 020-8652 8987
Website: www.caterer.com

Centre for Accessible Environments
Nutmeg House
60 Gainsford Street
London SE1 2NY
Tel: 020-7357 8182
Fax: 020-7357 8183
Email: info@cae.org.uk
Website: www.cae.org.uk

Chartered Institute of Patent Agents (CIPA)
95 Chancery Lane
London
WC2A 1DT
Tel: 020-7405 9450
Fax: 020-7430 0471
Email: mail@cipa.org.uk
Website: www.cipa.org.uk

Chartered Institute of Taxation
12 Upper Belgrave Street
London SW1X 8BB
Tel: 020-7235 9381
Fax: 020-7235 2562
Email: post@ciot.org.uk
Website: www.tax.org.uk

Chartered Insurance Institute (CII)
40–48 High Road
South Woodford
London E18 2JP
Tel: 020-8989 0464
Fax: 020-8530 5032
Email: customerserv@cii.co.uk
Website: www.cii.co.uk

Commission for Racial Equality (CRE)
St Dunstan's House
201–211 Borough High Street
London SE1 1GZ
Tel: 020-7939 0000
Fax: 020-7939 0001
Email: info@cre.gov.uk
Website: www.cre.gov.uk

Committee of Scottish Clearing Bankers
Drumsheugh House
38 Drumsheugh Gardens
Edinburgh EH3 7SW
Tel: 0131-473 7770
Fax: 0131-473 7799
Email: info@scotbanks.org
Website: www.scotbanks.org

Companies House (England and Wales)
Crown Way
Cardiff CF1 3UZ
Tel: 029-2038 8588
Fax: 029-2038 0900
Email:
enquiries@companieshouse.gov.uk
Website:
www.companieshouse.gov.uk

Companies House (Scotland)
37 Castle Terrace
Edinburgh EH1 2EB
Tel: 0131-535 5800
Fax: 0131-535 5820
Website:
www.companieshouse.gov.uk

Companies Registry (Northern Ireland)
IDB House
64 Chichester Street
Belfast BT1 4JX
Tel: 028-9023 4488
Fax: 028-9054 4888

Competition Act Enquiry Line
Tel: 020-7211 8989
Email: enquiries.competitionact@
oft.gov.uk

Consumer Credit Trade Association (CCTA)
Suite 8, The Wool Exchange
10 Hustlergate
Bradford BD1 1RE
Tel: (01274) 390380
Email: info@ccta.co.uk
Website: www.ccta.co.uk

Countryside Agency
John Dower House
Crescent Place
Cheltenham
Gloucestershire GL50 3RA
Tel: (01242) 521381
Fax: (01242) 584270
Email: info@countryside.gov.uk
Website: www.countryside.gov.uk

Croner's
Croner House
145 London Road
Kingston upon Thames
KT2 6SR
Tel: 020-8547 3333
Fax: 020-8547 2638
Email: info@croner.cch.co.uk
Website: www.croner.co.uk

Customs & Excise National Advice Line
Tel: (0845) 010 9000
Website: www.hmce.gov.uk

Department of Transport
Great Minster House
76 Marsham Street
London SW1P 4DR
Tel: 020-7944 8300
Website: www.dft.gov.uk

Department of Trade & Industry (DTI)
Enquiry Unit
Department of Trade and Industry
1 Victoria Street
London SW1H 0ET
Tel: 020-7215 5000
Fax: 020-7222 2629
Website: www.dti.gov.uk

Direct Marketing Association (UK) Ltd
DMA House
70 Margaret Street
London W1W 8SS
Tel: 020-7291 3300
Fax: 020-7323 4165
Email: dma@dma.org.uk
Website: www.dma.org.uk

Disability Discrimination Act Helpline
Tel: (0845) 762 2633
Website: www.disability.gov.uk

Disability Rights Commission
DRC Helpline
Freepost MID 02164
Stratford-upon-Avon
CV37 9HY
Tel: (0845) 762 2633
Fax: (0845) 777 8878
Email: enquiry@drc-gb.org
Website: www.drc-gb.org

DTI Business in Europe Hotline
Tel: 020-7215 8885
Fax: 020-7215 8884

DTI Consumer Safety Publications
Admail 528
London
SW1W 8YT
Tel: (0870) 150 2500
Fax: (0870) 150 2333

DTI Export Explorer
Tel: 020-7215 8885
Website: www.dti.gov.uk/ots

DTI Publications Orderline
Tel: (0870) 150 2500

DTI Small Business Service Loan Guarantee Unit
Department of Trade and Industry
Small Firms Division
Level 2, St Mary's House
c/o Moorfoot
Sheffield S1 4PQ
Tel: 0114-259 7308
Fax: 0114-259 7316
Email: trm.rimmington@sfsh-sheffield.dti.gov.uk
Website: www.dti.gov.uk

DTI's UK Online for Business
Website:
www.ukonlineforbusiness.gov.uk

DTI Trade Partners UK
Kingsgate House
66–74 Victoria Street
London SW1E 6SW
Tel: 020-7215 5444
Fax: 020-7215 4231
Website:
www.tradepartners.gov.uk

DTI TradeUK
Applied Psychology Research Ltd
Evergreen House
160 Euston Road
London NW1 2DX
Tel: (0870) 733 3323
Fax: (0870) 730 0731
Website: www.tradeuk.com

Dun and Bradstreet Europe Ltd
Holmers Farm Way
High Wycombe
Bucks HP12 4UL
Tel: (01494) 422000
Fax: (01494) 422260
Email: customerhelp@dnb.com
Website: www.dnb.com

E-centreUK
1 Kingsway
London WC2B 6AR
Tel: 020-7655 9000
Email: info@e-centre.org.uk
Website: www.e-centre.org.uk

Employee Ownership Scotland (EOS)
Scotland Online
Gateway East
Technology Park
Dundee DD2 1SW
Tel: (0845) 270 0027
Email: eos@sol.co.uk

Employers' Helpline
Tel: (0345) 143143
Tel (freephone): (0845) 607 0143
Government helpline offering free initial advice to new small businesses on PAYE, statutory maternity pay, VAT, and National Insurance contributions

English Partnerships
110 Buckingham Palace Road
London SW1W 9SA
Tel: 020-7881 1600
Fax: 020-7730 9162
Email: info@englishpartnerships.co.uk
Website: www.englishpartnerships.co.uk

Equal Opportunities Commission
Arndale House
Arndale Centre
Manchester M4 3EQ
Tel: (0845) 601 5901
Fax: 0161-838 1733
Email: info@eoc.org.uk
Website: www.eoc.org.uk

Euler Trade Indemnity plc
1 Canada Square
Canary Wharf
London E14 5DX
Tel: 020-7512 9333
Fax: 020-7512 9186
Website: www.eulergroup.com

Euro Preparations Unit
Tel: (0845) 601 0199
Website: www.euro.gov.uk

Exhibition Bulletin
Tarsus Martex
Commonwealth House
2 Chalk Hill Road
London W6 8DW
Tel: 020-8846 2700
Fax: 020-8846 2801
Website: www.e-bulletin.com

**Export Credits Guarantee
Department (ECGD)**
2 Exchange Tower
Harbour Exchange Square
London E14 9GS
Tel: 020-7512 7000
Fax: 020-7512 7649
Website: www.ecgd.gov.uk

**Federation of Recruitment and
Employment Services Ltd**
(See Recruitment and
Employment Confederation)

**Federation of Small Businesses
(FSB)**
Sir Frank Whittle Way
Blackpool Business Park
Blackpool
Lancashire FY4 2FE
Tel: (01253) 336000
Email: ho@fsb.org.uk
Website: www.fsb.org.uk

**Finance & Leasing Association
(FLA)**
Imperial House
15–19 Kingsway
London WC2B 6UN
Tel: 020-7836 6511
Fax: 020-7420 9600
Email: info@fla.org.uk
Website: www.fla.org.uk

Financial Services Authority
25 The North Colonnade
London E14 5HS
Tel: 020-7676 1000
Consumer helpline:
(0845) 606 1234 (local rate calls)
Fax: 020-7676 1099
Website: www.fsa.gov.uk

Gerling NCM
Capital Waterside
3 Harbour Drive
Cardiff CF10 6JH
Tel: 029-2082 4951
Fax: 029-2082 4003
Website: www.gerling.com

Grocer Marketing Directory
William Reed Publishing Ltd
Broadfield Park
Crawley RH11 9RT
Tel: (01293) 613400
Fax: (01293) 403108
Website: www.foodanddrink.co.uk

**Health and Safety Executive
Infoline**
Tel: (0870) 154 5500
Website: www.hse.gov.uk

Home Office Employers' Helpline
Tel: 020-8649 7878

HSE Books
PO Box 1999
Sudbury
CO10 6FS
Tel: (01787) 881165
Fax: (01787) 313995
Website: www.open.gov.uk/
hse/hsehome.htm

IFA Promotion
17–19 Emery Road
Brislington
Bristol BS4 5PF
Tel: 0117-971 1177
Fax: 0117-972 4509
Website: www.unbiased.co.uk

Industrial Common Ownership
Finance Ltd (ICOF)
227c City Road
London EC1V 1JT
Tel: 020-7251 6181
Fax: 020-7336 74077
Email: icof@icof.co.uk
Website: www.icof.co.uk

Industrial Common Ownership
Movement (ICOM)
Holyoake House, Hanover Street
Manchester, M60 0AS
Tel: 0161-246 2959
Fax: 0161-831 7684
Email: icom@icom.org.uk

The Insolvency Service
21 Bloomsbury Street
London WC1B 3QW
Tel: 020-7291 6895
Website: www.insolvency.gov.uk

Instant Muscle (IM) Ltd
Springside House
84 North End Road
London W14 9ES
Tel: 020-7603 2604
Fax: 020-7603 7346
Email:
headoffice@instantmuscle.org.uk

Institute of Chartered Accountants
in England and Wales(ICAEW)
PO Box 433
Moorgate Place
London EC2P 2BJ
Tel: 020-7920 8100
Fax: 020-7920 0547
Website: www.icaew.co.uk

Institute of Chartered Accountants
of Scotland (ICAS)
CA House
21 Haymarket Yards
Edinburgh EH12 5BH
Tel: 0131-347 0100
Fax: 0131-347 0105
Email: enquiries@icas.org.uk
Website: www.icas.org.uk

Institute for Complementary
Medicine
PO Box 194
London SE16 1QZ
Tel: 020-7237 5165 (answering
service only)

Institute of Export
Export House
Minerva Business Park
Lynch Wood
Peterborough PE2 6FT
Tel: (01733) 404400
Fax: (01733) 404444
Email: institute@export.org.uk
Website: www.export.org.uk

Institute of Practitioners in
Advertising (IPA)
44 Belgrave Square
London SW1X 8QS
Tel: 020-7235 7020
Fax: 020-7245 9904
Website: www.ipa.co.uk

Interactive Media in Retail Group
(IMRG)
5 Dryden Street
London WC2E 9NW
Tel: (0700) 039 4674
Email: market@imrg.org
Website: www.imrg.org

*International Chamber of
Commerce (ICC)*
ICC United Kingdom
14–15 Belgrave Square
London SW1X 8PS
Tel: 020-7823 2811
Fax: 020-7235 5447
Email: info@iccorg.co.uk
Website: www.iccwbo.org

Invest Northern Ireland
64 Chichester Street
Belfast BT1 4JX
Tel: 028-9023 9090
Fax: 028-9049 0490
Email: info@investni.com
Website: www.investni.com

Invest.uk
Email: invest.uk@dfi.gsi.gov.uk
Website: www.invest.uk.com

Lawyers for your Business
Freepost
PO Box 61
London NW1 0YP
Tel: 020-7405 9075
Fax: 020-7691 2007

Mailing Preference Service (MPS)
DMA House
70 Margaret Street
London W1W 8SS
Tel: 020-7291 3300
Fax: 020-7323 4165
Email: dma@dma.org.uk
Website: www.dma.org.uk

*Mail Order Protection Scheme Ltd
(MOPS)*
18a King Street
Maidenhead
SL6 1EF
Tel: (01628) 641930
Fax: (01628) 637 112
Email: enquiries@mops.org.uk
Website: www.mops.org.uk

Money Management Register
Tel: 0117-976 9444

*National Business Angels Network
(NBAN)*
Third Floor
40–42 Cannon Street
London EC4N 6JJ
Tel: 020-7329 2929
Fax: 020-7329 2626
Info pack hotline: 020-7329 4141
Email:
info@nationalbusangels.co.uk
Website:
www.nationalbusangels.co.uk

National Computing Centre
Oxford House
Oxford Road
Manchester M1 7ED
Tel: 0161-242 2200
Fax: 0161-242 2400
Email: enquiries@ncc.co.uk
Website: www.ncc.co.uk

*National Minimum Wage
Enquiries*
Freepost PHQ1
Newcastle upon Tyne
NE98 1ZH
Tel: (0845) 600 0678
Fax: (0845) 845 0360 (for leaflets)
Website: www.dti.gov.uk/ir/nmw

**Northern Ireland Bankers'
Association**
Stokes House
17–25 College Square East
Belfast BT1 6DE
Tel: 028-9032 7551

**Office for Harmonisation in the
Internal Market (Trade Marks and
Designs)**
Avenida De Aguilera 20
03080 Alicante
Spain
Tel: (0034) 96 513 9100
Fax: (0034) 96 513 9173
General fax: (0034) 96 5131344
Info fax: (0034) 96 5139173
Email: information@oami.eu.int
Website: www.oami.eu.int

**Office for National Statistics
(ONS)**
Press and Information Division
Government Building
Cardiff Road
Newport NP9 1XG
Tel: (01633) 812973
Fax: (01633) 812599
Email: info@ons.gov.uk
Website: www.ons.gov.uk

**Office of the Information
Commissioner**
Wycliffe House
Water Lane
Wilmslow SK9 5AF
Tel: (01625) 545745
Notification tel: (01625) 545740
Fax: (01625) 524510
Email: data@dataprotection.gov.uk
Website:
www.dataprotection.gov.uk

Office of Fair Trading
Fleetbank House
2–6 Salisbury Square
London EC4Y 8JX
Tel: 020-7211 8000
Fax: 020-7211 8800
Website: www.oft.gov.uk

**Office of Fair Trading
Consumer Credit Licensing Branch**
Craven House
40 Uxbridge Road
London W5 2BS
Tel: 020-7211 8608
Fax: 020-7211 8605
Website: www.oft.gov.uk

Office of Fair Trading Publications
OFT
PO Box 366
Hayes UB3 1XB
Tel: (0870) 606 0321
Fax: (0870) 607 0321
Website: www.oft.gov.uk

Patent Office
Concept House
Cardiff Road
Newport NP9 1RH
Tel: (0845) 950 0505
Fax: (01633) 814444
Email: enquiries@patent.gov.uk
Website: www.patent.gov.uk

**Patent Office Search and Advisory
Service**
Concept House
Cardiff Road
Newport NP9 1RH
Tel: (0845) 950 0505
Fax: (01633) 811020
Email:
commercialsearches@patent.gov.uk

Performing Rights Society
29–33 Berners Street
London W1T 3AB
Tel: 020-7580 5544
Website: www.mcps-prs-
alliance.co.uk

Periodical Publishers Association
Queen's House
28 Kingsway
London WC2B 6JR
Tel: 020-7404 4166
Fax: 020-7404 4167
Email: info1@ppa.co.uk
Website: www.ppa.co.uk

Phonographic Performance Ltd
1 Upper James Street
London W1R 3HG
Tel: 020-7534 1000
Email:
postmaster@ppluk.demon.co.uk

The Prince's Trust
18 Park Square East
London NW1 4LH
Tel: 020-7543 1234
Fax: 020-7543 1200
Email: printrust@princes-
trust.org.uk
Website: www.princes-trust.org.uk

**Recruitment and Employment
Confederation**
36–38 Mortimer Street
London W1N 7RB
Tel: 020-7462 3260
Fax: 020-7255 2878
Email: info@rec.uk.com
Website: www.rec.uk.com

Redundancy Payments Service
Helpline (0500) 848489
Website: www.dti.gov.uk

The Retail Directory
Newman Books
32 Vauxhall Bridge Road
London SW1V 2SS
Tel: 020-7973 6402
Website: www.h-info.co.uk

**Royal Institute of Public Health
and Hygiene**
28 Portland Place
London W1N 4DE
Tel: 020-7580 2731
Fax: 020-7580 6157
Email: ceo@riph.org.uk
Website: www.riph.org.uk

Royal Mail Sales Centre
35 Rathbone Place
London W1P 1HQ
Tel: (0845) 795 0950
Fax: 020-7239 2092
Website: www.royalmail.co.uk

Scottish Trade International
Scottish Enterprise
150 Broomielaw
Atlantic Quay
Glasgow G2 8LU
Tel: 0141-228 2808
Fax: 0141-228 2114
Website:
www.scottishdevelopmentinter
national.com

Shell LiveWIRE
Tel: (0845) 757 3252
Fax: 0191-261 1910
Website: www.shell-livewire.org

Showman's Directory
Lance Publications
Park House
Park Road
Petersfield
Hants GU32 3DL
Tel: (01730) 266624
Fax: (01730) 260117
Website: www.showmans-directory.co.uk

Simpler Trades Procedures Board (SITPRO)
Tel: 020-7215 0800 (helpdesk)

Small Business Gateway (Scotland)
Scottish Enterprise
150 Broomielaw
Atlantic Quay
Glasgow G2 8LU
Tel: (0845) 609 6611 ((0845) 607 8787 from outside Scotland)
Fax: 0141-228 2114
Website: www.sbgateway.com

Society of Pension Consultants
St Bartholomew House
92 Fleet Street
London EC4Y 1DH
Tel: 020-7353 1688
Fax: 020-7353 9296
Email: john.mortimer@spc.uk.com
Website: www.spc.uk.com

3i plc
91 Waterloo Road
London SE1 8XP
Tel: 020-7928 3131
Fax: 020-7928 0058
Website: www.3i.com

Technical Help to Exporters
British Standards Institution
Information Centre
389 Chiswick High Road
London W4 4AL
Tel: 020-8996 7111
Fax: 020-8996 7048
Website: www.bsi.org.uk

Telephone and Fax Preference Services
Haymarket House
1 Oxendon Street
London SW1Y 4EE
Tel: (0845) 070 0707/0702 (for telephone and fax preference registration respectively)
Tel: (01932) 414161 (information pack)
Email: tps@dma.org.uk

Trade International (Northern Ireland)
See Invest Northern Ireland

Wales Trade International
The National Assembly for Wales
Cathays Park
Cardiff CF10 3NQ
Tel: 029-2080 1046
Fax: 029-2082 3964
Email: exports@wales.gsi.gov.uk
Website: www.walestrade.com

Welsh Office
The National Assembly for Wales
Cardiff CF1 3NQ
Tel: 029-2082 5097

Workright Information Line
Tel: (0845) 600 0925 (for leaflet)

Index